1
Of The Late Bishop William W. Tucker

By

Frederick L. Cuthbertson

To Dr. Cowll,
May God grant you his loving grace!!
Ed. F.L. Cuthbertson

The "Sayings"

Of The Late Bishop William W. Tucker

By

Frederick L. Cuthbertson

Copyright © 1999 by Frederick L. Cuthbertson

All rights reserved. No part of this book shall be reproduced or transmitted in any form or by any means, electronic, mechanical, magnetic, photographic including photocopying, recording or by any information storage and retrieval system, without prior written permission of the publisher. No patent liability is assumed with respect to the use of the information contained herein. Although every precaution has been taken in the preparation of this book, the publisher and author assume no responsibility for errors or omissions. Neither is any liability assumed for damages resulting from the use of the information contained herein.

ISBN 0-7414-0515-6

Published by:

519 West Lancaster Avenue
Haverford, PA 19041-1413
Info@buybooksontheweb.com
www.buybooksontheweb.com
Toll-free (877) BUY BOOK
Local Phone (610) 520-2500
Fax (610) 519-0261

Printed in the United States of America

Printed on Recycled Paper

Published July, 2002

Table of Contents

Dedication 1

Preface 3

A Man for His Times 9

"Sayings" 25

Bibliographies 113

Reference Books 117

Acknowledgments 119

Dedication

This writing is dedicated to the memory and legacy of a man of God, that I've had the privilege to call my pastor, father, friend, and hero. Bishop William W. Tucker labored 27 years as the founding Pastor of Bethlehem Temple Apostolic Church in Philadelphia, PA, until his death in 1992. He was a Bible Teacher extraordinaire, and though his presence seemed intimidating and his voice, loud and gruff, he was a kind and generous man. Bishop used many sayings when speaking about walking with God, and some were quite humorous in his unique way of expressing them. I have compiled many of them in my memories, having been under his pastorate for 24 years. I believe the Lord has inspired me to put down in writing these "golden nuggets" of the wit and wisdom of a great man of God. My desire is to present them with my thoughts on their meanings, and give a scriptural reference concerning it. I hope and pray that those who read it will appreciate the knowledge that God blessed this man who loved God and his people.

Frederick L. Cuthbertson

Preface

The purpose of this book is given not only as a tribute to a man who greatly influenced my life, but as a tool for ministers, laity and the general public alike in the understanding of God and His Church. It provides a point of reference for discussion on the Bible by the believer and the unchurched, since the central theme is about relationships. Many pertinent issues are expressed through the quotations, comments and scriptural references of this book.

As a youth raised in the church, I've sat and listened to numerous sermons taught by Bishop Tucker on life in the church among the people of God. Having believed I've learned from his teachings, I experienced after his demise that his words took on a more profound influence in my life. When I began to personally endure situations in my relationships with fellow saints that turned indifferent after years of good fellowship, I was deeply hurt and wounded. It brought me out of my naivete concerning people, and supplied the reality that everyone professing Christ doesn't possess him.

Reminiscing on my past experiences, the sayings of my late Pastor reverberate through my mind as it reflected the very things that can occur when saints go contrary to sound doctrine. Like an open book, his words brought to light many things that I've only grasped before. Only when one goes through hardships can he truly understand and appreciate the truth of the scriptures.

Paul says in Romans 5:3 through 4th verse, "and not only so, but we glory in tribulations also; knowing that tribulation worketh patience; and patience, experience; and experience, hope." Spiritual growth and maturity comes as a result of going through unpleasant times and becoming a victor, rather than a victim. There are many in our churches today that are hurting, due to the carnality and misconduct of so-called professing Christians. Betrayal of trust by religious leaders and the laity have reached widespread proportions, and the secular world perceives the Church as a dying institution.

However gloomy the spiritual climate of the Church seems to be God has never left himself without a witness as he has raised those who will promulgate the Gospel of Jesus Christ. There are revivals being held throughout the nation, with preachers stirring up the consciousness of an immoral society to turn to God, and they of the Church to turn back to the Bible as their rule and guide of faith. By presenting a practical portrayal of the various types of relationships that takes place in church, I hope to address the misconceptions held by some who think that life in the church is an utopia of peace and harmony. In a perfect world that would be the desire of any believer, but we live in an imperfect and sinful world.

We are flawed and struggle daily with the contrary desires of the flesh, yet God in his infinite mercy has invested his Divine Word to creatures "made a little lower than the angels." Paul place such responsibility in it's proper perspective when he states in 2nd Corinthians 4:7,"but we have this treasure in earthen vessels, that the excellency of the power may be of God, and not of us."

One will note when reading this book, that the majority of the quotations and comments seem to imply a negative outcome concerning these relationships. This is not to say that this is typical among the people of God, on the contrary, it can be a wonderful and fulfilling life. When one searches the scriptures, he will find that in both the Old and New Testament, they who truly served God were usually in the minority; for example, in the book of Genesis, Noah being warned of God of the coming judgment on a wicked world built an ark for the preservation of his family. As the world perished by the Great Flood that consumed it, only eight souls were saved in the safety of the ark.

In Genesis 19th chapter is given the account of Lot and his family as they are instructed to leave the corrupt cities of Sodom and Gomorrah, before God's destruction of them. Upon leaving the doomed cities, Lot's wife, against the commands of God turned towards the burning catastrophes she saw and turned into a pillar of salt. Only Lot and his two daughters were left from the destroyed multitude. Of the gathering of the children of Israel who left Egypt to journey to the land of Canaan, only Joshua and Caleb survived from the first generation after forty years of wandering in the wilderness. The books of Numbers and Joshua tell of their exploits and faithfulness to God, as well as their allegiance to Moses.

In the 7th chapter of Judges, Gideon called by God to lead his people against the Midianites is told that he had too many with him to achieve the goal of defeating the enemy. So as a test, God instructs him to decree to the people that they who are fearful and afraid can depart, and twenty two thousand responded, leaving ten thousand. God decreases the number further by bringing them to the water and declaring that whoever lappeth water as a dog to be set aside. Only three hundred men did so and went on to defeat the Midianites.

In the New Testament, Jesus in his Sermon on the Mount discourse says in Matthew 7:13-14th verses, "Enter ye in at the strait gate: for wide is the gate, and broad is the way, that leadeth to destruction, and many there be which go in thereat: Because strait is the gate, and narrow is the way, which leadeth unto life, and few there be that find it." He further states in Matthew 20:16,"So the last shall be first, and the first last: for many are called, but few chosen." In the sixth chapter of John, we find Jesus telling the multitude that he is the "Bread of Life" and many among his own disciples being offended departed from him. When he turned to the twelve men personally chosen by him he asked them in verse 67,"will ye also go away?" Peter responds in the next verse, "Lord, to whom shall we go? thou hast the words of eternal life." Paul says in 1st Corinthians 1st chapter and 26th verse, "For ye see your calling, brethren, how that not many wise men after the flesh, not many mighty, not many noble are called. He concludes in the 28th verse by stating that the insignificant and despised of men has God chosen to bring to nothing what mankind esteems highly.

Peter in his epistle declares in 1st Peter 4th chapter, 18th verse, "and if the righteous scarcely be saved, where shall the ungodly and the sinner appear?" The consistent pattern throughout the scriptures clearly reveals that those who will be saved are far less than the majority who will be lost. Remember what Jesus said in Matthew 24:37-39th verses," but as the days of Noah were, so shall also the coming of the Son of man be. For as in the days that were before the flood they were eating and drinking, marrying and giving in marriage, until the day that Noah entered into the ark. And knew not until the flood came, and took them all away; so shall also the coming of the Son of man be."

This prophecy of Jesus clearly speaks of these turbulent times that we live in today, and there is no need to doubt that the same results will occur as they have in time past. Also, Jesus' parable about the sower, who sow seeds in the field as given in the book of Matthew, 13th chapter speaks of the distinct types of soil the seeds felled upon. They are described as the wayside, stony, thorns and good ground. Jesus uses these conditions to metaphorically illustrate the spiritual condition of man's heart in response to the word of God. Of the four, only the good ground produced positive results when receiving the seeds. In continuing with his teaching in the chapter, Jesus gives the parable of the wheat and tares. Here, he distinguishes the sower as himself, the wheat as the" children of the kingdom", and the tares as the "children of the wicked one."

The tares were planted by the Devil to corrupt the field, so that to gather them out to be destroyed would also affect the wheat at harvest time. The decision was to allow them to grow together and at harvest, separate them accordingly. He concludes in verse 49 by saying," so shall it be at the end of the world: the angels shall come forth, and sever the wicked from among the just." In keeping with

Jesus' teaching of the sower and they of the good ground being in the minority, there's no reason to doubt that the same holds true concerning the wheat and tares. In light of these truths I echo the words of Peter in 2nd Peter 3:11," seeing then that all these things shall be dissolved, what manner of persons ought ye to be in all holy conversation and godliness." In conclusion my prayer to God is, if one soul can be changed after the reading of this book, then it has accomplished its purpose.

Amen

Bishop Tucker:
A Man for His Times

Bishop William W. Tucker was a well-known preacher during his lifetime in the Pennsylvania, New Jersey and Delaware region. Although his resume may not compare on the same scale as other nationally known pastors of his era, he considered himself an ordinary man entrusted with an extraordinary calling. He took seriously and with firm conviction the responsibilities required for the task of pastoring God's people.

Bishop Tucker came from an era of pastors whose style of leadership was authoritative but benevolent towards the people. He would often say, "I will give you the shirt off my back in trying to help you, but if you do wrong I'm on you like white on rice." A visionary who strived to fulfill what God gave to him; those who followed his lead sometimes misunderstood his vision for the church.

Nevertheless, he assured the people and often said that he would never steer them wrong because God would punish him. His manner of preaching was quite demonstrative in that as he continued, his voice would rise and the word of God poured out in a rhythmic cadence. He would slam one of his hands hard upon the pulpit in sequence with his preaching emphasizing his point. Sweat flowed profusely down his face as he walked to both sides of the rostrum.

It was with a physically exhausting style of preaching that he ministered to the congregation, but he believed in giving the best of himself to God. Possessed of a pastor's heart, Bishop Tucker displayed genuine love and care for the people he led, and was generous in giving to the church of his substance rarely asking anything in return.

He enjoyed a personal rapport with many of his members calling them affectionately by nicknames he ascribed to them. Bishop Tucker had a quick humorous wit that lightened the atmosphere among the congregation while seriously ministering of the word of God. During casual settings he would often talk about his early years in the church and the experiences he encountered while serving God.

The following pages will divulge some of those experiences that shaped the life of Bishop William Wilbur Tucker, and the impact he had on all who came in contact with him. William Jr. was born March 19th, 1911 in Philadelphia, Pennsylvania to William and Berda Tucker. His father made his living as a railroad laborer while his mother remained at home to manage things between young William and his brothers and sisters.

The family lived in the Tioga section of Philadelphia. As a youth, William attended Kennedy Elementary School and eventually left school by the time he reached the eighth grade. William's teen years after dropping out of school were spent cavorting with friends.

One day while attending the Rose of Sharon Church at Tenth and Thompson Street, he came under conviction when hearing the word of God. Feeling like a condemned criminal, he realized the need to be saved and consented to be baptized in the name of Jesus Christ and received the Holy Ghost. He was seventeen at the time.

Thankful for the renewed life in Christ, William became a quick study in understanding the Bible, receiving the preached and taught word by the pastor, Elder I. C. Hall. Elder Hall had succeeded the founding pastor of Rose of Sharon Church, Elder Basden. Inquisitive, William was a good Sunday school scholar, always asking questions in Bible class. Often, Elder Hall had to say "sit down Brother

Tucker and let someone else answer." During the 1930's the country was suffering the pains of the Great Depression, and times were difficult, jobs scarce and making a living hard.

Despite the hardships there was a great sense of community and fellowship being enjoyed by the "saints" of God. They called one another by this term based after the Apostle Paul's addressing believers in his salutations as found in his epistles. This was characteristic among Pentecostal churches of that day. Because many didn't have cars to go to church, they walked even though it took a number of miles to get there. The saints would walk in groups, meeting others along the way to church, and after service follow the same pattern in going home.

On Sunday, church services would be an all-day affair starting with Morning Prayer, followed with breakfast, Sunday school, Morning Worship and then dinner. At dinner the young people would set the tables for the ministers and adults as they ate first. Sometimes it would take longer for the adults to finish; being preoccupied in conversation, but none among the young people dared to openly complain for fear of incurring the wrath of the church mothers who sat nearby.

Afternoon service would convene, followed by Street service outside the church and ended with Night service. It was not unusual for the saints to return home after midnight, with some having to go to work a few hours later. During these simpler times, there was little fear of danger when walking the streets at night. In the summertime, it was not unusual for residents to leave doors and windows open to get some relief from the humid nights.

Neighborly kindness and courtesy were extended among the residents as they looked out for each other and their children. The same spirit of communion was also in the church as fellow saints took a genuine interest in each other practicing Paul's admonishment, "look not on your own things but also on the things of others." With the young people, every mother in the church was as much a guardian as one's own mother and the same held true with the men as father figures.

Respect for all adults in the church was strictly required of the young with no exception and quick discipline was administered to any who would misbehave in church. Now, a young man William continued to grow spiritually in the Lord and was appointed to the Deacon Board proving his faithfulness in serving the needs of the church. Although circumstances were difficult for William during those times, he made do with what little he had.

With only one suit in his possession, using a necktie for a belt to hold up his pants and stuffed paper in his shoes to cover the worn holes in them, William faithfully attended church. He persevered knowing that in due time God would bless him for his faithfulness. He made a living at the time working in a cigar factory. William continued to grow in the Lord and gain knowledge of God's word until he responded to God's call to the ministry. Eventually he was elevated in the ministry as an Elder, well seasoned in the Word of God. His desire to preach was so strong that sometimes he could be found preaching to the coals in the basement while shoveling them in the furnace to provide heat for the home during the winter.

Elder Tucker began to take interest in a young sister in the church by the name of Pauline Hall. She was one of several daughters of the Pastor, who was active in the church singing and directing the choir. They began to date and to learn that they shared mutual feelings for each other. Elder Tucker asked Pastor Hall for Pauline's hand in marriage and he gave them his blessings.

On July 20th, 1938, William Tucker and Pauline Hall were united in Holy Matrimony. Shortly after, the country was forced into World War Two. Many were called into service and Elder Tucker was no exception. He was inducted into the Army Air Corps as a conscientious objector due to his religious belief in not taking arms for the purpose of killing. This was an unpopular stance to take during such a troubled time, but Elder Tucker held fast to his convictions.

He was often ostracized for his stand and transferred to a number of camps for preaching the word of God to fellow soldiers. Branded a troublemaker for his activities, he was given the most dirty and menial jobs to do, but this did not break his resolve. At one camp, he was transferred away because the commanding officer's concern was "if we keep this man here he'll have all my men to be like him."

On another transferred assignment when Elder Tucker met his commanding officer, the officer immediately threatened him by saying, "if you come here with that preaching mess you're going to the stockade." Elder Tucker firmly responded, "Well Sir, have it open for me because if God wakes me in the middle of the night and tells me to preach, I'm preaching." In time the officer eventually respected Elder Tucker and prior to his next transfer to another camp, the officer spoke highly of him to the fellow soldiers saying, "I wish I had more men like him."

Despite the frequent transfers to various camps, such movements were really blessings in disguise for it opened doors to preach in many churches near the camps, most of them in the South. He preached fervently to many, telling them of the death, burial and resurrection of Jesus, baptism in Jesus' name and the infilling of the Holy Ghost, speaking in tongues as the Spirit gave utterance. He baptized one man in the river near one of the camps, while others were blessed through his ministry. He was truly a soldier in the Army of the Lord.

In all, Elder Tucker was stationed in eleven different camps in the service and was honorably discharged. Upon returning to Philadelphia, he gained employment at the Philadelphia General Hospital as an orderly and remained there until his call to the pastorate. Elder Tucker was a stickler on being to work on time, so much so that he would arrive there a few hours before hitting the clock. He continued this habit in the church as a pastor as he would be praying, reading the Bible and preparing himself to receive the saints when they entered in.

Prior to his pastoral calling he developed an acute condition in his throat from years of hard preaching and went to a specialist to have it diagnosed. The doctor grimly told him that he had cancer and should immediately cease from preaching. Elder Tucker, responding in a weak whispering voice said, "Doctor, in due time I'll be talking normal just like you." The doctor's reply was, "it will take a miracle, Reverend." Elder Tucker held to his faith and trusted God to heal him from this condition.

One day a friend, Elder Raymond Moore stopped by to see Elder Tucker. He had been praying and fasting for a month and told Elder Tucker about how the Lord sent him to come pray for him. Placing his hand on his throat, Elder Moore called on the name of Jesus. His hand felt like fire on Elder Tucker's throat that after the prayer, he felt his throat clearing to be able to speak above a whisper. There was great rejoicing that day.

Returning to the doctor he was checked out again and to the doctor's amazement he declared, "Reverend, your throat is healing rapidly." Remembering Elder Tucker's promise that he'll speak normal again, the doctor conceded by telling William, "you pray for me, Reverend." Elder Tucker was active in the Greater Pennsylvania State Council of the Pentecostal Assemblies of the World, and served faithfully in many capacities.

When the Lord moved on Elder Tucker to start a church, he shared his desire with Elder Hall and he gave Elder and Sister Tucker his blessings. Although Sister Pauline was excited to venture out to this new work, she had mixed feelings leaving her father's church and the two choirs she directed. Knowing that it was only right to follow her husband, she accepted the challenge of being a supporter of his ministry.

They purchased a storefront on the corner of 32nd and Diamond Street as the place to start this work and opened it in March of 1965. They named the church Bethlehem Temple and the opening day speaker was District Elder Stephen Bright, Pastor of Zion Apostolic Temple of Philadelphia. The theme of his message was "An Open Door." The church was filled to capacity with many, friends and dignitaries to witness the grand opening.

When the festivities were over and the people had departed, Elder and Sister Tucker were left with the reality that there was much work to be done. Soon, members were added to the church and although growth was slow, Elder Tucker preached as though he had hundreds. The early members included the Roach family, Mother Flora Barclay, Deacon Levi Moore and his wife Sister Kate Moore.

The Tuckers lived nearby in an apartment above a doctor's office on 32nd and Page Street and those early years were a struggle keeping the church and home above water. There were times when all they had to eat was some pretzel rods and a container of water in the refrigerator to drink. On one occasion in church during a hot summer day, Elder Tucker, discouraged because he had few members requested that the entrance door remain closed. Sister Tucker, miserable from the heat, stood up and said to her husband, "open the door, everybody outside knows you don't have many people, it's hot in here."

Elder Tucker, knowing his wife was right, sheepishly complied with her wishes and left the door open to receive some relief from the heat. It made him realize that circumstances however unpleasant can't be allowed to dampen one's spirit when serving God. Being the only minister at the time, Elder Tucker provided all the preaching and teaching in the church while his wife directed the musical part, playing the piano, singing and leading devotion and prayer service.

On many Saturdays Elder Tucker would clean the church in preparation for Sunday services. Being a hard worker most of his life, it was not beneath him to maintain the upkeep of the church even though he was the pastor. Concerning service he would say", God never called a lazy man to do his work."

Between 1968 and 1970, the Lord began to add an influx of people to Bethlehem Temple as groups of families entered in. Families such as the Cuthbertsons, Greens, Gordons, Coopers, Fords, and the Bigelows. Elder Tucker's prayers were being answered as the Lord sent in people who helped to build and established Bethlehem Temple as a growing church.

Elder Tucker was a great Bible teacher who loved to expound the word of God to the people. Tuesday night was Bible class and his approach in delivering the word was straight and plain. When making a point in his teaching Elder Tucker would often make facial gestures when he knew somebody reacted negatively to his words. Though it seemed comical to see his expressions, he was serious in what he taught and was unfazed as to whether the saints accepted it or not.

His stand on living the Christian life was dogmatic on some issues and did not sit well with some of the members; the same held true with fellow pastors who fellowshipped with him. A saying went out about him from among the churches who knew him which said, "if you don't want to live right, don't go to Tucker's church, because he's too hard."

His response would be, "I can't be any harder than the Word and the way of the transgressor is hard." Because of Elder Tucker's serious demeanor when ministering in church, some people misunderstood him. He was intolerant of misconduct in the church and would at times openly rebuke the guilty party, yet when alone he would cry over them. There were times when he publicly apologized to the congregation if he felt his words too harsh when reproving them.

Elder Tucker was a man who wasn't ashamed to express emotion and feelings to the people. He often testified that despite his reputation as being a hard man, deep down he was a big crybaby who cared about the people of God. He lived up to his responsibilities as a pastor, visiting the sick in hospitals and those who were in need. Never interested in driving a car, he took public transportation in his many travels to see the saints and handle church business. He and his wife purchased a car to make traveling easier for the both of them in doing missionary work for the church.

On one occasion Elder Tucker, who had a unique way with words announced to the church that the "greatest speaker in Pentecost" was coming and to make sure that everyone attend so as not to miss this great event. Many saints expressed excitement wondering with one another, who is this "greatest speaker" and where is he from? There was great expectation for this "celebrity" to the extent that on that particular night everyone was dressed in his or her Sunday best outfit for the occasion.

With the saints now seated and anticipating this person to arrive, Elder Tucker stood up and announced, " you can now receive the greatest speaker in Pentecost by going down on your knees and shout Hallelujah until the Holy Ghost speak out of you." Taken back initially by Elder Tucker's statement, the saints obeyed and soon after the Lord came through filling many with his Spirit that night.

Although Bethlehem Temple was growing in numbers, the building where they worshipped was beginning to deteriorate and it was becoming intolerable to stay. Elder Tucker spearheaded a building fund drive to purchase a new place to worship.

Elder Tucker, always one to provide a lighthearted message, posted a sign saying, " Don't dance and shout until after you pay your Building Fund Pledge." After searching a few places, Elder and Mother Tucker settled on a building located at 123-25 South 51st Street adjacent to Samson Street. It was formerly a firestation called the Second Alarmers, and now it would become a "spiritual firestation" for the Lord. Settlement was made in September of 1972. Just a month prior to the settlement, Bethlehem Temple became incorporated as a church and was renamed, Bethlehem Temple Apostolic Faith Church, Inc.

While the saints worked to clean and prepare the building for the grand opening that was scheduled for the Sunday after Thanksgiving Day, the heater in the basement of the building broke down. There were fears that the scheduled opening would be delayed if the heater were not fixed on time. Elder Tucker called for the saints to come out on Thanksgiving Day to give a prayer of thanks for God blessing them with the new place of worship.

Sensing the fears and doubts on the faces of the people because of a possible delay of the opening, Elder Tucker summoned the people to gather around him and he preached faith to them, assuring them that come Sunday the church would open as scheduled. That day the building was still empty, no carpet laid or pews aligned in place. The rostrum had not yet been built and no heat to feel warmed; yet Elder Tucker's words echoed in the people ears that there would be church on Sunday.

The next two days went like a whirlwind as all the problems were being solved as Elder Tucker promised. The carpet came and was laid, a new heater installed and the pews that were held in storage long before a building was found for worship were set in place. On Saturday the rostrum was built and completed and the pulpit set in its place.

On Sunday, November 26, 1972 the grand opening of the new building took place as scheduled and was filled to the extent that there was standing room only. Pastor Helen Campbell of Pentecostal Faith Assembly Church in Philadelphia was honored as the opening day speaker. She was a long time friend and colleague of the Tuckers who had worshipped together with them in the days of their youth at Rose of Sharon.

Her scripture text was taken from the book of Psalms 2nd division and first verse which reads, "Why do the heathen rage and the people imagine a vain thing?" It was a stirring message followed by an inspiring call to discipleship by Elder Fred Barnaby, Pastor of Philadelphia Tabernacle Church. The success of the grand opening proved to be a blessing for the church as souls continued to come and hear the unadulterated Gospel of Jesus.

Now settled in the West Philadelphia area, Elder Tucker stressed the need for the saints to evangelize the neighborhood to attract people to come to church. Many Saturdays were spent with the saints canvassing the neighborhood, passing out tracts or witnessing to passersby about the "good news" of Jesus. Elder Tucker would say in regard to evangelizing that" sheep beget sheep" and, "if you bring in the fish I'll clean them through the Word."

Unlike most pastors who sit in the middle seat behind the pulpit, Elder Tucker's seat of choice was the last seat on the left side of the rostrum. His reason was to have a full view of the congregation and to discern the spirit of the people like a shepherd who observes the condition of his sheep. Being one who disliked a dull service, his keen sense of perception could tell that something was amiss among the people. He would frequently remark that the "Devil is sitting cross-legged in here" and lead the saints in praising God and prayer until there was a breakthrough.

His stout stature was an imposing sight to behold when preaching the word under the "anointing" of God; yet during light moments he was down to earth and accessible to all who came in contact with him. The Lord blessed the Tuckers to move from their apartment to a home. Elder Tucker was a determined man when it came to setting goals and completing them. An early project was changing the front of the building from its old firehouse appearance to a church front appropriate for its present use.

A contractor was secured and a style selected to beautify the church's front exterior. By example he inspired the saints to contribute to the cost of the work by first giving of his own money to the cause. In a matter of months the work was completed and a beautiful white stone front was displayed for all to admire.

Elder Tucker was very independent when it came to matters of paying his way and not being in debt to anyone. He put in practice the scripture, " Owe no man anything." The same method he used when arriving to church well ahead of time was applied in paying his bills. He believed it was best to take care of financial obligations in advance, so he could have more time to address the spiritual needs of the church.

Having this drive moved him to help pay off the mortgage of the church ahead of schedule. Elder Tucker, after being a member of the Pentecostal Assemblies of the World for over forty years left the organization to join with another group. This organization was the Pentecostal Assemblies of Churches of Jesus Christ, headquartered in Havre de Grace, Maryland.

Making new acquaintances and fellowships with affiliated churches in the organization provided a welcomed experience for Bethlehem Temple. The churches in Maryland began to learn what they in Philadelphia had known, that Elder Tucker was a mighty man of the scriptures. He was an excellent teacher of the mysteries and the revelations of the ages in the Bible as expounded by the noted Pentecostal preacher and writer, Bishop G. T. Haywood.

Elder Tucker would teach from the Biblical charts created by Bishop Haywood during the Bible class session of the State Council held quarterly each year. Both preacher and lay member sat spellbound, as Elder Tucker would explain the meanings of the illustrations given on the charts and their applications. In 1975, he was elevated to the office of bishop by Bishop Charles Johnson, the Presiding Bishop of the organization.

In 1978, Bishop Tucker desiring to start a radio ministry, purchased air time on a Camden, New Jersey station named WCAM 1310 A.M. (later renamed WSSJ). For a half-hour on Sunday evening at 6 p.m., people could tune in to hear a word of prayer, scriptural reading, and songs from the choir and preaching of the word from Bishop Tucker.

Prior to preaching, Bishop Tucker would open with a song entitled, "I've Got A Feeling Everything Is Going To Be Alright." This became his "signature song" whenever he would preach on the airwaves. He was gracious in allowing the associate ministers to preach on the broadcast. In time the radio format had increased to an hour and drew favorable responses from the listening audience by way of phone calls while the service was on the air.

He loudly declared the Gospel of Jesus Christ without fear or favor and emphatically professed that it was "Holiness or Hell" to the listeners. His zeal in proclaiming the Gospel truth was such that he would challenge anyone to come to the church after preaching on the air to prove him wrong. His words in making the challenge would be, "Come and get me!" There was none to take Bishop Tucker up on his challenge. Several members joined the church as result of his preaching on the air.

Bishop Tucker was one who didn't back down when debating the scriptures and on one occasion disputed with a relative of a member who happened to be a Muslim. The discussion was centered on Abraham and his sons, Isaac and Ishmael concerning who was the promised son of inheritance. When Bishop sensed the Muslim brother getting upset as the debate became heated, Bishop would hug him a few times to calm him. Eventually the brother conceded to Bishop Tucker, acknowledging his wisdom of the scriptures and departed amicably out of the church.

Bishop Tucker's unique manner of using sayings to illustrate the life of a believer was a featured part of his ministry. His anecdotal descriptions on the blessings or consequences of the daily walk of a Christian were sometimes humorous yet to the point in the truth being expressed.

On speaking against mistreatment of fellow saints he would quip, "people will Ku Klux you in a minute." The term "Ku Klux" was derived from the name of the notorious hate group, the Ku Klux Klan. Or when preaching on the subject of "sin", he sensing some of the members squirming in reaction to his words would say, I'm walking heavy today, hear me now!"

Concerning how one would be judged for eternity, Bishop Tucker would say, "a horse don't live his life as a horse then change into a mule at death." He further explained the point by saying, " the way you live is the way you die, if you died as a sinner that's how you will be judged." Such expressions came as a result of his experiences in the ministry and dealing with people through various situations.

Believing the turbulent times of the day as reflectively described in the Bible as the "last days", Bishop Tucker would urgently proclaim, "there's no time to stop and pick flowers." Also, another phrase indicative of those years by Bishop Tucker was" to look for anything to happen" regarding the conditions of the world.

In 1981, Bethlehem Temple became part of a fellowship of churches that held meetings twice a year. Pastor Eula M. Boggs-Yates from Elizabethtown, Kentucky sponsored the services and testified of coming to Philadelphia through a vision from the Lord to meet Bishop Tucker. She described the appearance of Bethlehem Temple and a physical condition that Bishop Tucker suffered from at that time. She proved to be a great help and support for Bishop and Mother Tucker as her healing and prophetic ministry relieved many of the saints.

Bishop Tucker was a strong advocator of supporting women ministries and gave his time and substance to see such ministries succeed. His generosity was also extended to the saints when going on sponsored trips as he would pay the costs for those who otherwise could not afford it. Being a man of faith, Bishop Tucker prayed for the saints afflicted with severe illnesses and God healed them.

On one occasion in 1981, a long time member, Evangelist Janie English was diagnosed with colon cancer that was in its last stages. During a Sunday morning service in November of that year, Bishop Tucker called Evangelist English to the front of the church. After praying for her, he assured her that if she believed God, she would be healed from her condition.

Two weeks later she learned that she was healed from the cancer as her doctor ran a series of tests that registered negative. Puzzled, the doctor knew from earlier diagnosis that the cancer was there, but now in light of the recent findings there was nothing. One year later, Evangelist English was blessed in having a baby girl on November 26, 1982.

On another occasion Mother Louise Green, mother of Evangelist English and a devoted senior member of the church was stricken with cancer. But Bishop prayed for her and God healed her from the cancer. In 1985, Bishop Tucker with the church joined briefly with the Holy Bethel Pentecostal Church of the Apostolic Faith Association, Inc. of Bethlehem, Pa. under the auspices of Bishop Henry Dorrah.

Soon after, Bethlehem Temple went independent as a church and in the waning years of Bishop Tucker's life his health began to deteriorate. No longer able to stand to preach but for a few minutes, the remainder of his sermon would be spent sitting down. His voice remained powerful, loud and clear ministering effectively to the people and exhorting them to live right for God. He often testified how

God promised him during his early struggles in the ministry that his last days would be his best days and God proved to be true to his word.

As a pastor who had concerns about the welfare of the church and his own mortality, Bishop Tucker would startle the congregation by saying on occasion "when I close my eyes, you're going to see something", referring to what would occur after his' death. Coming into 1992, Bishop Tucker was mostly confined to bed at home when his health prevented him from coming to church.

Though he suffered greatly in the last years of his life, Bishop Tucker never complained or asked for sympathy. His last appearance at the church was Sunday, April 5, 1992. Confined to a wheelchair and obviously weak, he nevertheless exhorted the congregation to be strong and in the power of God's might.

The following Sunday on April 12th with his faithful wife and companion by his hospital bedside Bishop William W. Tucker passed this life to be with the Lord leaving a great number of sayings that express the essence of the man.

"Sayings"

1. "IT'S TIGHT, BUT IT'S RIGHT"

Bishop Tucker had a delivery when preaching the word that is best described as cut and piercing, and not pleasing to the flesh. He reminded us that to make it to heaven requires full obedience to God's word, slipping and sliding just won't do.

Scripture References
Jeremiah 23:29
Hebrews 4:12

2. "A FORWARD CAT, GETS HIS HEAD CRACKED"

Sometimes in our haste to do things, we act before we think and fall into trouble. The saying, " curiosity killed the cat, " refers to one not minding their own business, and becoming a "busybody" in other men's matters. It brings problems unexpectedly in one's life.

Scripture References
Proverbs 25:12
II Thessalonians 3:11
1 Timothy 5:13

3. "MEAN WHAT YOU SAY, AND SAY WHAT YOU MEAN"

In a time of much irresponsibility and denial of what is said, whether it is from high officials or common people, the need to be truthful and honest is essential for the child of God. The saying goes, "You're only as good as your word, " and one's character is often judged by whether or not he lives up to his word. A person who makes bold and declarative statements, and never acts on them becomes small in the eyes of others, and his' word becomes meaningless. He is no longer to be trusted.

Scripture References
Proverbs 8:8-9; 15:23
St. Matthew 12:36

4. "PROCRASTINATION IS THE THIEF OF TIME"

We fall into problems unnecessarily when putting off things that need immediate attention. Whatever has to be done for the present cannot wait until tomorrow, because there's no promise we will live to see it.

Scripture References
Proverbs 27:1
James 3:5

5. "THE WAY UP WITH GOD, IS DOWN"

If one desires to be blessed of God, he must learn to be of a humble spirit for God does not call the proud and haughty. People who are vain and full of themselves can never be used effectively by God. Their pompous attitude gets them in constant quarrels with others.

Scripture References
Psalms 24:4
Proverbs 11:2; 13:10; 16:18; 21:4

6. "WHAT YOU DO IN HASTE, YOU'LL REPENT IN LEISURE"

Decisions that are made without proper counsel or through stubbornness can lead to many disappointments. Acting impulsively or on a spur of the moment brings disaster and heartache to one who follows such a path.
Some decisions may affect a person for a day; others like getting married can last a lifetime. Woe to the one who made the wrong decision, for he has a lifetime to regret it.

Scripture References
Proverbs 14:29; 29:20
Ecclesiastes 5:2; 7:8-9
Hebrews 12:16-17

7. "FOOLS RUSH IN, WHERE ANGELS FEAR TO TREAD"

Like No. 6, this statement deals with doing things hastily without thought. A fool is not one who is mentally deficient or lacks intelligence, but is driven by carnal desires that leads to constant trials due to unwise decisions. Bishop said when a person lives in the flesh; he's liable to do anything an unsaved man would do.

Scripture References
Proverbs 12:15-16; 14:9,17; 18:6-7; 20:3

8. "FLATTERY WILL GET YOU NOWHERE"

Flattery is defined as praising one too much in an insincere way in order to win favor with that person. Flatterers are shrewd manipulators and opportunistic in their pursuit of "preying" on victims for personal gain. They use their "gift of gab" to influence people to believe they're well thought of, as well as luring them into false security with "acts of kindness." Such people are like a "slithering snake in the grass, " winding themselves around their prey, squeezing the life out of them. Excessive flattery leads to plain lying, and once they're exposed their fortunes tumble like a stack of cards.

Scripture References
Job 32:21-22
Psalms 5:9; 12:3; 78:36
Proverbs 20:19; 26:28; 29:5

9. "NO ONE DOES WRONG AND GET BY"

When saints decide to follow the wrong path, and ignore the word of God, they suffer dire consequences as a result. There are those who become stiff-necked and hard-hearted and feel they could do anything without giving an account of their actions. It catches up to them in the long run, as they reap what they sowed.

Scripture References
Proverbs 1:22-32; 13:15; 29:1,6
Romans 6:23

10. "WHATEVER YOU DO, BE HONEST"

This was the most quoted saying that Bishop Tucker preached and taught, for if one couldn't be honest with himself, he will not be with God or with people. Uprightness and sincerity is a must for every child of God, and to do less is living beneath one's privileges.

Scripture References
Psalms 26:11
Proverbs 11:3; 20:7
Romans 12:17; 13:13
Philippians 4:8
Hebrews 13:18

11. "IF YOU MAKE YOUR BED HARD, YOU HAVE TO LIE IN IT"

Similar to No. 6 and 7, this saying involves making decisions against better judgment, and suffering the pain of accepting the consequences. Regretfully when one acts on emotions rather than practical principles, disappointments usually is the result.

Scripture References
Proverbs 3:5; 11:14; 13:15; 14:12; 28:26
Isaiah 47:8-11

12. "DON'T READ ON THE LINE, BUT READ BETWEEN THE LINE"

It is sad that virtues like honesty and sincerity are in short supply in today's society, and even in the church it is found lacking among the saints. People won't give straight answers, but try to hide what they mean by double-talk and subtlety. They fail to see that the spiritual-minded person can discern through the camouflage and determine their falsehood.

Scripture References
Psalms 12:4-5; 52:2-4
Proverbs 14:15
I Corinthians 2:15
Hebrews 5:12-14

13. "DON'T GIVE THE DEVIL A BASEBALL BAT TO HIT YOU WITH"

Once God saves a person, the Devil declares war on him and is determined to bring one back under his power. He looks for signs of weakness and opportunities to take advantage of a believer, when they're not vigilant. We must strive to always be conscientious, for if we give in to our flesh, the Devil is there to embarrass us and make us ashamed.

Scripture References
II Corinthians 2:11
Ephesians 4:27; 6:11-18
James 4:7

14. "SOME PEOPLE CAN'T STAND PROSPERITY"

Bishop Tucker's teaching on this subject was that it is better if some people remain poor for the drastic change in personality that occurs when they become blessed with material things. When they had nothing they faithfully attended church, gave liberally of what little they had, and were pleasant to everyone. But once blessed, they're too busy for church, too stingy to give, and act ugly when approached. We were reminded to "never forget where God brought you from."

Scripture Reference
St. Matthew 6:19
St. Luke 12:15-21
I Timothy 6:6-11
James 5:1-6

15. "THE DEVIL SITTING CROSSLEGGED AMONG YOU"

When a congregation is not on one accord whether in worship or spiritually in relationship to one another. This was a phrase that Bishop used in describing the situation. God's blessings cannot be received if the people are not together. One who stops praying and being led of the Spirit makes himself an easy prey for the Devil.

Scripture References
Proverbs 14:34; 29:18
II Timothy 2:25-26

16. "GETTING TIRED OF HYPOCRITING"

The problem with hypocrisy is that when things are seemingly going right as a result of being pretentious, like a drug, it lures one into false security. Thinking he's got it made through his deception, life suddenly takes a turn for the worse; he becomes miserable trying to maintain a positive front before others. Two choices await him, confess and get right with God, or leave the church and live the life of a sinner. We must be real when serving God.

Scripture References
Job 20:5-29
Proverbs 11:9; 23:7; 26:25
St. Matthew 23:28
Hebrews 11:25
I Peter 2:1

17. "FOLK ARE FOLK, AND GOING TO BE FOLK"

It's a universal fact that people regardless of race, creed, or national origin share many similar traits and responses in their relationships. We're neither angels nor devils, but humans made in the image of God and right or wrong will react the same no matter the situation.

Scripture References
Psalms 8:4-6; 139:14
Acts 17:24-26
Romans 10:12

18. "DON'T BE A GARBAGE CAN FOR ANYBODY"

Talebearers and gossipers are major disruptions in the church; those who love the Lord should steer clear of them. The saying, "a dog that brings a bone will carry one, " aptly describes such persons who indulge in this kind of mischief. They have no concern about the welfare of the church.

Scripture References
Proverbs 11:13; 17:9; 18:8; 26:20-28
I Peter 4:15

19. "WALK WITH GOD IN THE SUNSHINE, HE'LL BE WITH YOU IN THE RAIN"

The Christian walk is often misconstrued as a problem free existence and easy to live by. The reality of the scriptures tells us otherwise; there are hardships and suffering in the life of one that walks with God. The word gives us the assurance that God will never leave us during hard times.

Scripture References
Psalms 23rd and 27th chapters
St. Matthew 18:20; 28:20

20. "NO SWEETHEARTIN' IN THE CHURCH"

Bishop Tucker was a staunch advocate of the sanctity of marriage; divorce was not in his vocabulary. He stressed the need of couples reconciling together when problems arise, and telling them there's nothing too hard that the Holy Ghost can't solve. "Sweethearting" as he called it refers to those who carry extramarital affairs, and singles who indulge in long-term relationships with no intentions of marrying one another. Such activities are clearly against God's word and bring a reproach to a church.

Scripture References
Proverbs 6:24-33; 23:26-33; 30:20,23
Malachi 2:14-16
Matthew 5:27-28
Romans 7:1-3
I Corinthians 6:15-20; 7:1-3,8-14,27-28
Hebrews 13:4

21. "MORE NERVES THAN A BRASS MONKEY"

This phrase speaks of one who is stubborn, ornery, and arrogant and refuses to hear instruction on what's right. Such a person runs headlong into disaster with no regard to himself or others.

Scripture References
Proverbs 29:1
Ecclesiastes 8:11-13
I Timothy 6:3-5

22. "TRYING TO BE A MISS ANN"

A person, who is vain, proud, and pompous, fits the description of this term given by Bishop. One who is materialistic, and possesses a smug attitude towards others will have many difficulties entering God's kingdom.

Scripture References
Proverbs 14:3; 16:8,18-19; 21:4; 28:25
II Timothy 3:1-5
I John 2:16

23. "YOU CAN JUMP AS HIGH AS BILLY PENN'S HAT, BUT WHEN YOU COME DOWN LIVE HOLY"

The term illustrates the need to live right when serving God, and how singing, dancing or shouting is meaningless without a godly life being reflected. Bishop Tucker used the statue of William Penn atop the City Hall Tower as a metaphor to show the danger of being inconsistent in our lives.

Scripture References
Ecclesiastes 5:1
St. Luke 6:46
Romans 2:1
Titus 1:16
James 3:10

24. "TAKE CARE OF THE HANDS, YOU DON'T KNOW WHOSE HANDS YOU MIGHT FALL INTO"

The teaching here was concerning how saints ought to treat one another as saints. Jesus' saying, "as you would that men should do to you, do you also to them, " is meant in a positive and godly way. The Bible tells us that what you sow that shall you also reap; mistreatment of a fellow saint can only bring bad repercussions at reaping time. You could fall in the hands of one who shows no mercy as a result of being unkind to another. Don't dish out what you can't take.

Scripture References
Job 4:8
Proverbs 6:14; 16:28; 22:8
Hosea 8:7
Galatians 6:7-8

25. "TWO TYPES OF PEOPLE GOD DON'T CALL"

According to Bishop, they're "lazy" and "stingy people" that God will not call to build his kingdom. They're hangers-on who are stumblingblocks to the growth of a church. Excuse making and complaining seems to be their expertise, and they bring a foul spirit to any service.

Scripture References
Proverbs 11:26; 18:9; 19:24; 21:25; 24:30-34; 25:19
Ecclesiastes 10:18
James 2:5-8, 14-16

26. "LOOKING SPIT-EYED AT SOMEBODY"

Facial expressions and body language tell a lot about what's going on in a person, that words can't convey. Harboring hostilities towards anyone is unbecoming as a saint of God, and like the saying "what's in you will soon come out of you." We should always present a pleasant countenance.

Scripture References
1 Samuel 18:7-9
Proverbs 23:6-7
Isaiah 33:15
St. Matthew 5:29
St. Mark 7:22
St. Luke 11:32-34

27. "KINFOLK SALVATION"

It's amazing that people who are the most critical of the "wrongs" of others, are so lenient when the same wrongs are found among members of their own family. The true test of a believer is not standing for God in the midst of a sinful world, but in the confines of one's own home. There's no greater "peer pressure" than the one exacted by a family who holds an opposing view from the one who trusts God. We cannot compromise the standard of God to please our loved ones, when they are wrong.

Scripture References
Genesis 37:1-28

Leviticus 19:15
Deuteronomy 27:19
Amos 3:3
St. Matthew 10:34-40
St. Mark 3:31-35
St. John 7:1-5
I Timothy 5:27-28
I John 3:8, 10

28. "PEOPLE DO WHAT THEY WANT TO DO"

No matter how much preaching and teaching a church receives there's always a segment of people who march to the beat of their own drum. Nothing seems to move them to "spruce up" spiritually, and they have a schedule all their own when coming to church. Some are pleasant and others downright uncouth.

Scripture References
Psalms 9:17
Proverbs 12:15; 13:13,15,18,20; 14:9,12
Romans 1:18-32
Hebrews 10:25

29. "IT'S TOO LATE WHEN THE DEVIL GET'S YOU"

As a follow-up to No.28, this phrase deals with the aftermath of what occurs to an individual who disregards God's word. Some will repent and get their lives right with God, but others having become self-willed and hardened lead to a tragic end.

Scripture References
Romans 1:21-32; 8:5-9,12-15
Ephesians 4:17-19; 5:5-8
II Peter 2:3

30. "CROOKED AS RIDGE AVENUE IS STRAIGHT"

People, who spend their time living carnally, will never grow in the Lord. Being dishonest and conniving can only bring shame to the one following this contrary path. Like Ridge Avenue their lives take winding turns instead of a straight path.

Scripture References
Psalms 125:5
Proverbs 2:12-15; 4:19
Hebrews 12:12-13

31. "LET ME SEE YOUR MOTIONS, TRA, LA, LA, LA, LA"

We are familiar with the saying that, "actions speak louder than words "and truly if a saint of God wants to maintain a good name they must "do" and not just "say."
Talking a good talk without a "good walk" will not sway the discerning person from knowing that you're not sincere in what you say.

Scripture References
Proverbs 12:19,22
Ephesians 4:25
I Timothy 2:2
James 1:22-27
I Peter 2:12

32. "YOU LOVE ME? PROVE IT! PROVE IT!"

The word "love" has been much maligned today and haphazardly tossed about in our conversation. The true meaning has been lost due to carnality and worldliness, and many relationships have broken up because of it. There is a selfish spirit among us that is misleading people to believe that as long as they're on the receiving end of being treated right, that's love. They don't feel obligated to reciprocate in kind, and get insulted if you don't meet their satisfaction. The Bible speaks of the "agape" or godly love we should have for one another. A well-known poem reads "love isn't love unless it's given away."

Scripture References
St. Matthew 22:39
St. John 13:35; 15:12
Romans 12:9
I Corinthians 13th chapter
Ephesians 6:24

33. "MAKING HEAVEN TOO HIGH, AND HELL TOO HOT"

Sometimes in our zeal to witness to people about salvation, we can become harsh and judgmental in attitude of presenting Christ to them. Hellfire sermons don't move people as they did in time past, and imposing upon sinners to behave as saints is futile. Christ gave the best example in his showing love to the people, and they responding to his word. We must display the same spirit.

Scripture References
Proverbs 12:25; 15:23; 25:11

Isaiah 50:4
St. John 4:7-30
St. Matthew 9:35-36
I Corinthians 4:20

34. "GONE TOO FAR, STAYED TOO LONG, AND CAN'T GET BACK"

The plight of the backslider is never pleasant, and when he comes to himself and wants to get right with God, often it's too late.

Scripture References
Proverbs 14:14
Isaiah 1:4
St. Matthew 24:12
St. Luke 9:62; 11:26
Galatians 4:9
II Timothy 3:13
Hebrews 12:15-17
II Peter 2:20

35. "STRIKE WHILE THE IRON'S HOT"

It's best to take advantage of opportunities that will help you in being blessed when presented. Putting off till another time may not be wise, for some opportunities come once in a lifetime, and if missed can bring heartache to the one who lost out.

Scripture References
Proverbs 10:22; 11:3, 5, 8,17,31; 22:9

36. "BETTER TO BUY A TOY AT THE FIVE AND DIME AND PLAY WITH, THAN TO PLAY WITH GOD"

If there's ever a time to be real for God its now, with the immorality, hypocrisies, and contentions going about in the churches today. There's no time Bishop used to say to "stop and pick flowers, " but to "get down" to the reality of serving God. Playing church is not the answer and putting on a form of godliness will not justify one before God.

Scripture References
Ephesians 5:5-7
II Thessalonians 2:10-12
Hebrews 12:29
II Peter 2:12- 22

37. "USING THE CHURCH LIKE A SPIRITUAL ASPIRIN TABLET"

Similar to No.36, this phrase shows how people who are lukewarm in spirit will display piety and sanctimony in worship to appear "righteous" before men. They're hypocritical and deceitful in nature, and deceived in believing that coming to church makes them right. All they're doing is soothing their guilty consciences.

Scripture References
Job 8:13; 27:8
Isaiah 9:17
St. Matthew 6:2, 5, 16; 23:24-28
James 3:14-17

38. "SANCTIFIED PEOPLE ARE THE MEANEST, FILTHIEST, AND LOW-DOWN PEOPLE ON THE FACE OF THE EARTH"

This harsh statement made by Bishop Tucker has been for years the most difficult for me to accept. Being naive and young in the Lord, I've thought everyone who is saved was striving to live right like myself. But as the years went and I matured by my experiences dealing with people, I've learned that my most grievous moments came at the hands of saints. One learns that his greatest hurts will come in the church, rather than the world.

Scripture References
Job 16:20; 19:19
Psalms 41:9; 55:12-15
Micah 7:6-8
Zechariah 13:6
II Corinthians 11:26
II Timothy 4:16

39. "DON'T LIVE IN A CRAMP, GO TO HELL CADILLAC STYLE"

There are no real benefits trying to live a double life, and putting up a façade to impress people. You can't have the world and the church too; if one wants the pleasures of the world, it's better to go all the way with the world, than to live in a "strait" in church. Enjoy all the luxuries of life since the judgment of God will be your end.

Scripture References
Psalms 49:10-14
Proverbs 23:5; 27:24
Ecclesiastes 2:10-11

St. Matthew 6:24
St. Mark 4:19
St. Luke 16:19-31
I Timothy 6:9-11

40. "EAT THE FISH, BUT DON'T SWALLOW THE BONES"

Anyone who has eaten fish with bones and accidentally swallowed some, knows how unpleasant it is when it causes one to choke. As saints of God we're reminded to "eat" the word of God, and avoid false doctrines and philosophies of men. Eating the wrong things such as gossiping and hearsay can also impede one's spiritual growth.

Scripture References
Job 23:12
Jeremiah 15:16
St. Matthew 16:6-12
Galatians 2:4
Colossians 2:8
II Peter 2:1-2

41. "IF YOU RUN FROM THE LION, THE BEAR WILL GET YOU"

Usually when failure to do what is necessary takes place, we tend to shun responsibility for our actions. When calamities come as a result of our negligence, instead of acknowledging our faults, we cover them. Hiding It only leads to other problems that soon overwhelms us. The phrase "Honesty is the best policy" still rings true today.

Scripture References
Proverbs 11:21
Jeremiah 11:11

Amos 5:19; 9:2-4
I Thessalonians 5:3
Hebrews 2:3; 12:25

42. "SMILING IN YOUR FACE, BUT STABBING YOU IN THE BACK"

As saints of God, we are taught to trust and love one another, and unlike our past life in the world, we drop our defenses in relating to each other. Unfortunately when one becomes carnal, he can inflict great harm to the saint who has trusted him. People need to realize that to hurt a fellow saint, is to hurt Christ, for we are members of the same body. The consequences can be severe to the offender.

Scripture References
St. Matthew 25:41-46
St. Luke 17:1-2
I Corinthians 8:9-12
Galatians 5:12-13; 6:7-8
II Thessalonians 1:6
Hebrews 2:1-3; 6:4-6

43. "TRYING TO PULL HEN'S TEETH"

Describing the difficulty of getting people to understand God's word or to live right; can indeed be like pulling "hen's teeth" since hens don't have any. One can't be made to live right. People who are stubborn and self-willed dig themselves into a snare that they can't get out of.

Scripture References
St. Luke 16:13
James 1:8
Jude 4,8,10-13

44. "LAY DOWN WITH DOGS, RISE UP WITH FLEAS"

Being associated with persons who are carnal and unsavory will only stifle the walk of one whose intentions are to please God. Whether they're friends or relatives, if God is not top priority in their lives, they can only bring you down. These have ruined many a good reputation of saints who were sincere, and they should be avoided at all costs.

Scripture References
Psalms 1:1
Proverbs 4:14; 22:24; 23:6-7; 24:1; 28:7; 13:20
I Corinthians 5:11
Ephesians 5:11-12
I Timothy 5:22

45. "PLAY WITH THE DEVIL, HE'LL KILL YOU"

In war, corroborating with the enemy carried a severe penalty for an offender, even death. When saints "fool around" with the devil's tools and indulge in worldly pursuits and pleasures, it leads to disaster for the victims. Like the saying, "if you dance to the music, the piper must be paid."

Scripture References
St. Luke 21:34-36
II Corinthians 11:3,13-15
I Thessalonians 5:1-4
I Peter 5:8

46. "SCALDING A MONKEY WITH ICE WATER"

This odd-sounding phrase given by Bishop Tucker, was his way of describing slick and smooth talking individuals, who connive their way among the saints. They seek personal gain and positions through the Church by craftiness and cunning, and are convincing in the things they pronounce to win people over. Great care and discernment must be exercised to "weed" them out.

Scripture References
Psalms 101:5
Ecclesiastes 8:11-13
Romans 3:13; 16:17-18
I Corinthians 2:4
II Corinthians 12:20-21
I Peter 2:1
II Peter 2:18-19
Jude 16

47. "BE CAREFUL WHO YOU TALK TO ABOUT SOMEBODY, HE MAY BE THAT PERSON'S FRIEND"

James, in his epistle writes about the dangers of an untamed tongue and the damage it can cause to one afflicted by it. Those who are carried away with gossip, rumors, and hearsay have ruined a reputation. Many have been wounded or left the church due to the insensitive conduct of such people who bring division, instead of harmony. Discretion should be invoked before a statement is said about anyone, and consideration to the person being talked to.

Scripture References
Proverbs 11:9,12-13; 12:18
Ephesians 4:31; 5:11-12
Titus 3:2
James 4:11
I Peter 2:1

48. "DON'T HAVE A LEG TO STAND ON"

The problem with saints who follow the carnal path is, to do and live right carries responsibilities they're not willing to measure up to. They rather wallow in the muck and mire of mediocrity and hide in the midst of the congregation, thinking there is none to notice. Sooner or later their sin catches up and exposes them before all with no excuse.

Scripture References
Joshua 6:18; 7th chapter
Job 15:34
Psalms 1:5; 26:5
St. Luke 14:18
Colossians 3:25
I Timothy 5:23

49. "ENDING UP BEHIND THE EIGHT BALL"

Making unwise decisions without understanding the situation can lead to many problems. Better to listen to one who's been through similar experiences to help you avoid such troubles.

Scripture References

Psalms 10:5; 50:17-21
Proverbs 9:6,9; 15:31-32
St. Luke 8:15
James 1:19; 4:17
Revelation 2:11

50. "A BAD HAIRCUT IN THE DEVIL'S BARBERSHOP"

This was the theme to one of many sermons preached by Bishop Tucker, dealing with the story about Samson and Delilah. The book of Judges, chapters 16 and 17, tells us how the Philistines paid Delilah to learn the secret of Samson's great strength. After much persistence, he succumbed to her charms and revealed his secret, and while asleep, she cut his locks of hair and rendered him helpless. He was then made an "object" of ridicule before the Philistines. The lesson tells us we must be ever vigilant, or the Devil will likewise "strip" us of our power.

Scripture References
Proverbs 7:6-27
St. Matthew 26:41
St. Luke 8:13
I Corinthians 10:13

51. "IF YOU STAND UP, GOD WILL SHOW UP"

In the midst of test and trials, the believer must persevere in order to become strong in the Lord. To be fainthearted only gives the enemy the means to overtake and defeat you.

Scripture References
Judges 7:1-3
Proverbs 24:10

Isaiah 40:29-31
St. Luke 18:1
II Corinthians 10:3-6
Galatians 6:9
Ephesians 6:10-18

52. "THERE'S JUST AS MUCH SIN WEARING A LONG DRESS, AS IT IS A SHORT ONE"

Modesty of dress as Paul writes to Timothy in I Timothy 2:9, is defined as that which is proper and decent. Though a church has the prerogative to enforce a "dress code" for its members, problems arise when more attention is given to "appearance" than the "conduct" of the people. A church can become judgmental and self-righteous in attitude towards anyone that doesn't conform to their way of thinking. Jesus was concerned about the condition of a man's heart, and not what he wears.

Scripture *References*
I Samuel 16:7
St. Matthew 6:25; 7:15; 23:23-26
St. Luke 20:46
St. John 2:24-25; 7:24
Romans 14:1-5,17
I Timothy 3:15
I Peter 3:3-4

53. "IT'S A BARNUM AND BAILEY WORLD; AS PHONY AS IT CAN BE"

In the entertainment world, things are created to amuse, excite or titillate the senses. Events are advertised on the order of being spectacular to lure people in to see it, and illusions mesmerize others to believing that things are not what they appear to be. Likewise in church, things can be not what they appear, as there are "acts and performances" being done just like in a circus.

Scripture References
Psalms 101:7
Proverbs 27:6
Jeremiah 17:9
St. John 15:19; 17:9,16
I Corinthians 2:6-8; 7:31
II Corinthians 11:13
James 4:4
I John 2:15-17

54. "YOU CAN'T GET NOTHING OUT OF IT, UNLESS YOU PUT SOMETHING IN IT"

In the sowing and reaping principle, what you plant will produce a harvest that can be good or bad depending on how you planted the seed. One can't expect an abundance of fruits, if he plants nothing.

Scripture References
St. Matthew 13:3-23
II Corinthians 9:6,11
James 3:18

55. "EVERYBODY CAN'T BE TELLING THE SAME LIE"

When there's a disturbance among the sheep, a groaning sound can be heard among the fold indicating trouble. In a church an undercurrent of problems can be known by a number of individuals that may be denied by others. You can be sure if more than one is seeing the same thing, it's bound to be true.

Scripture References
Deuteronomy 17:6
Proverbs 14:5,25; 19:28
St. Matthew 18:16

56. "IF EVERYONE PLEADS HIS OWN CASE, NO ONE WOULD BE HUNG"

The lack of taking responsibility for one's actions, is an increasing problem in today's church. Instead of humbling himself to confess wrong, he either blames others or rationalizes his error. Trying to save "face" in light of blatant wrong is useless.

Scripture References
Proverbs 12:15, 19, 23; 30:12-13
Isaiah 5:21

57. "IT"S EITHER HOLINESS OR HELL"

Bishop Tucker was dogmatic when it comes to God's truths, and "holiness" was one of them. Holiness is not a denomination, but the very nature of God and what he requires of his people. The scriptures are clear on the choices one must decide on where he spends eternity.

Scripture References
Romans 6:22-23
II Corinthians 7:1
Hebrews 12:14, 25-29
I Peter 1:15-16

58. "THAT DON'T AMOUNT TO A HILL OF BEANS"

Too often the thing we should be concerned about is neglected, and we get involved in matters that prove to be of no value to us. As saints we must put our priorities in proper order, starting with God and then with others.

Scripture References
Psalms 127:1-2
Proverbs 3:5-6; 13:15
Ecclesiastes 2:10-11
St. Matthew 6:25-34

59. "PEOPLE WILL TELL YOU ANYTHING, IF THEY THINK YOU'RE DUMB"

It is often said "you can't judge a book by its cover, "and truly first impressions of a person can be assumed without knowing that person. People who maintain a carnal perception can misjudge someone based on appearance, speech, or that person's disposition. They think nothing of saying whatever foolish thing comes to mind, and are shocked to find the one who they feel is "simple" knows that they're "hypocrites."

Scripture References
I Samuel 21:11-15
Psalms 38:12-22; 119; 122
Proverbs 14:31; 22:16
St. Matthew 5:3, 5
II Corinthians 10:7
James 2:1-4,9

60. "PEOPLE LOVE TO BE LIED TO"

When saints are walking with God, hearing the word of God is a delight, even if it shows them when they're wrong. But if they slip into a carnal mode, the word becomes irritating and uncomfortable. Soon their ears are "itching" for hearing false and misleading messages that can only harm their spiritual life. They become blind to that which is right.

Scripture References
Jeremiah 6:10; 7:4
St. Matthew 15:14
St. John 3:19; 9:39-41
Romans 8:5-9; 16:17-18
II Corinthians 4:3-4
Ephesians 4:17-19
II Timothy 3:1-7; 4:1-4
II Peter 1:5-10

61. "TAKING KINDNESS FOR WEAKNESS OR STUPIDITY"

Like No. 59, there are those following the worldly mentality of judging virtues such as kindness or goodness, as a sign of weakness. They think such people are easy to take advantage of and "used" for their selfish aims. Mistreatment of any saint, particularly one that does right can only bring a reaping of chastisement to the offender.

Scripture References
Job 4:8
Proverbs 6:14; 16:28; 22:8
Malachi 2:10; 3:5
St. Matthew 18:5-7
Romans 12:9-10, 14, 16-21

62. "DON'T COME THROUGH THE BACK DOOR"

As a pastor, Bishop Tucker had the responsibility of leading, feeding and counseling the saints on their problems. He considered it a disservice for any saint to go to someone not designated or qualified rather than to him. As he said , " I'm the one watching for your souls, " and to go to another raised suspicions of "hiding" a matter from him. Saints must be honest with their pastor if they want to be helped.

Scripture References
I Timothy 3:1-7; 5:1, 17-20
Hebrews 13:7, 17
I Peter 5:1-4

63. "SHOUT 'EM SWEATY AND ROLL 'EM DIRTY"!

This was a phrase Bishop Tucker used to describe the need of the saints getting involved in worshipping and praising God in service. "It's not the time, " he would say, to sit there looking "cute or sophisticated." One should let go of his pride as to how well he's dressed, and yield to the Spirit. Some would shout, others dance and still more saints praised God as it pleased them. There 's no concern about what one's wearing when "God is in the building."

Scripture References
II Samuel 6:14-22
Psalms 100; 1-2, 4; 149:1-5; 150:3-6

64. "TIME IS THE GREATEST FORTUNE TELLER"

There are situations and circumstances that are difficult to understand at present, and depending on the severity of them, it can be enough to make one give up. Patience to endure will allow one to give God the means to work things out in His time and for the good of the believer. In contrast, to the person, who walks contrary, events in time can only lead to his ruin.

Scripture References
Psalms 89:47
Ecclesiastes 3:1, 17; 9:11
Hosea 10:12
Romans 8:28; 13:11

65. "I CAN'T BE HARDER THAN THE WORD"

Because Bishop Tucker's style of preaching was often cut and piercing, there were those who thought his delivery was "too hard" to take. His defense was that he couldn't do more or less than what the word of God says. Also he exhorted us that as the "messenger" of God for the people, for one to be offended at him was to feel the same towards God.

Scripture References
II Chronicles 20:20
Isaiah 58:1; 62:6-7
Jeremiah 1:8-10; 6:17-19
II Corinthians 4:1-2

66. "DON'T LET THE BEE STING YOU IN THE SAME PLACE TWICE"

There's a saying that tells us that "we are to learn from our mistakes." Sometimes in this Christian walk, we tend to forget past errors and fall in the same troubles again. It's one thing to make a mistake in a situation you're not aware of, but to know it and commit it again is indeed foolish.

Scripture References
Proverbs 13:16-17; 14:15-16; 24:16
St. Luke 11:24-26
Galatians 2:18
James 4:17

67. "WON'T GIVE A CRIPPLE A CRUTCH TO LEAN ON"

Selfishness and insensitivity towards any saint are major stumblingblocks to the one who claims to know God. Withholding the opportunity to help others is clearly a sign of immaturity and carnality, and such a one forfeits the blessings of God in his life. Being kind to the unsaved for the purpose of impressing them with your "spirituality, " yet indifferent with the saints is also deceitful.

Scripture References
Proverbs 3:27-29; 11:24-26; 21:3; 24:11-12
Romans 12:11-13

Galatians 6:10
Philippians 2:2-5

68. "IF YOU LET THE DEVIL FAN YOU TO SLEEP, YOU'LL MISS SOMETHING"

Staying alert to hear the word of God is a necessity for the child of God who wants the best for his soul. Just as natural sleep puts one in a state of unconsciousness from outward activities, the Devil can lure a saint into the same state spiritually through worldliness.

Scripture References
St. Luke 21:36
I Corinthians 10:12; 16:13
Colossians 4:2
I Thessalonians 5:5-6
I Peter 5:8
Revelation 3:2, 11; 16:15

69. "PEOPLE CAN KILL YOU WITH THEIR TONGUE, AS WELL AS USING A GUN"

The third chapter of the book of James gives a very graphic illustration concerning the destructive power of the tongue. Many reputations have been ruined by those who are carried away with the misuse" of what they say about people. The word is clear concerning God's "disgust" for this activity and it is a self-destructive trait to have. There's a true saying that reads" hatred does more damage to the vessel in which it is stored than it does to the object upon which it is poured." Such are they that are "ruled" by their tongue.

Scripture References
Job 20:12
Psalms 34:13; 39:1; 101:7; 120:7
Proverbs 10:31; 12:19; 13:3; 18:21; 26:20-26,28
I Timothy 3:8
James 1:26

70. "MORE LIES TOLD IN A TESTIMONY SERVICE, THAN DOWN AT CITY HALL"

As a follow-up to No. 69, dishonesty and pretension can be found even in the most sacred of functions, such as in a praise service. I've found in my years of serving God that some who express lengthy spiritual testimonies, are the most contentious and mean-spirited of people in church. They do it to make others believe they're so "spiritual, " and for the purpose of "competition."

Scripture References
I Samuel 15:13-23
Job 15:34
Psalms 51:16-17
Proverbs 21:3-4, 16
Ecclesiastes 5:1-2
Isaiah 1:11
St. Matthew 23:14, 28
St. Luke 18:9-14
Titus 1:15-16

71. "I'VE GOT YOUR JOY IN MY POCKET"

Being a pastor committed to telling the truth, Bishop Tucker's messages did not always sit well with people. He, knowing this, made it plain to all that he would not "sugarcoat" the word to please anybody and they who are not receptive to the word, make themselves miserable.

Scripture References
I Kings 22:5-18
Proverbs 13:13, 15, 18
Acts 7:51-54
Romans 2:3-9
II Peter 2:10
Revelation 3:17

72. "GOD CAN USE A SHARP SWORD, BETTER THAN A DULL ONE"

Though Bishop Tucker did not complete formal training in school, God blessed him with an abundance of knowledge of the Bible. He gained wisdom through the experiences of dealing with all walks of life. Nevertheless he encouraged the saints to further their education in becoming productive citizens, as well as effective in God's ministry.

Scripture References
Proverbs 16:24; 17:27-28; 25:11
Ecclesiastes 10:12; 12:11
Isaiah 50:4
I Corinthians 2:1-8
Titus 2:8

73. "YOUR SALVATION STARTS IN YOUR BEDROOM"

With the crises of marital problems and breakdowns of relationships in the church, one cause is the lack of understanding God's place in the home. Many think their salvation is confined within the sacred halls of a church, and life is lived outside as it pleases them. Our spirituality begins in the most intimate of situations between a man and wife. When God is left out of the picture, then the same problems afflict a saved couple as one in the world. Charity begins at home then spreads abroad.

Scripture References
Proverbs 5:18-20
Ecclesiastes 9:9
I Corinthians 7:1-5, 10-16, 27-29
Ephesians 5:22-33

74. "IT TAKES A BIG MAN TO ADMIT HE'S WRONG"

One of the best features of Bishop Tucker, was his ability to "humble" himself when he made a mistake or wronged someone. He did it publicly, before all and to an individual if it was done privately. The people respect leaders more when they see graciousness displayed.

Scripture References
Proverbs 16:19; 22:4; 29:23
Isaiah 57:15
Romans 12:3
James 4:10
I Peter 5:5

75. "WHY DIE LIKE A FOOL"

King Solomon, the Bible says was the wisest man that ever lived with the exception of Jesus himself. He had power, fame, wealth and peace during his reign in Israel. He built a great temple in dedication to God, and was feared by the surrounding nations. But later in life he gave in to his carnal appetites, married many women and introduced much idolatry in Israel. He died in shame and caused Israel to split apart. If it could happen to Solomon, then surely it will to us if we follow the same downward path.

Scripture References
Proverbs 12:15
Ecclesiastes 2:4-11; 7:17; 8:11-13
St. Luke 12:16-21
Romans 1:18

76. "TWO WORDS WILL KEEP US OUT OF HEAVEN, FORGIVE ME"!

Disagreements and disputes will sometime occur between saints, but the danger is carrying grudges and refusing to forgive someone. We must keep in perspective that as God forgave us we must do likewise.

Scripture References
Psalms 32:1
St. Matthew 6:12-15:18:35
Ephesians 4:32
I John 2:12

77. "WORRY GIVES YOU TWO THINGS; MORE WORRY AND A QUICK GRAVE"

Anxiety over problems, either by our faults or circumstances beyond our control; can hurt us physically and spiritually. We must learn how to trust God, and let him take care of the situation.

Scripture References
St. Matthew 6:25-34
St. Luke 10:41; 21:34
Philippians 2:6
I Peter 5:7

78. "GOD'S LITTLE HELPER"

This follow-up to No. 77 describes how impatient we can be concerning God, when it comes to solving our problems. Being hasty or impulsive in trying to "fix" a problem that you feel is taking God "too long, " can only bring disaster.

Scripture References
Proverbs 14:29; 19:2-3
Ecclesiastes 5:2; 7:8-9
James 1:3-5

79. "WON'T LIVE RIGHT TO SAVE YOUR LIFE"

Many a pastor has experienced the frustrations of travailing with saints, who no matter how much counseling and prayer they receive, trouble follows them continually. Like walking on a treadmill, they're in constant motion but getting nowhere. While you're "stressed out" being concerned about their welfare, they freely go about without a care in the world making a mess of their lives and others.

Scripture References
Proverbs 6:9-19; 11:3, 7; 13:13-15; 14:12; 25:19; 27:12;   28:13-14
Jeremiah 13:23
St. John 6:70-71
II Peter 2:10

80. "A MAN IS SAVED EVERYWHERE BUT HIS' PRIVATE PARTS"

This statement by Bishop Tucker was not meant as an indictment against men, but on a reality that is all too common with men. The "reining" in of our sexual urges is a daily struggle for most men, and the yielding to it has befallen even the greatest of men. Men such as Samson, David and Solomon accomplished great things in the service of God. But the same zeal and ambition that drove them to greatness, also brought them down when driven by carnal desires.

Scripture References
Judges 16th chapter
II Samuel 11th chapter
I Kings 11th chapter

Proverbs 5:3-20; 6:32-33; 7:7-27
St. Matthew 5:27-28, 31-32
Ephesians 5:5-6

81. "TWO WRONGS DON'T MAKE A RIGHT"

Rendering evil for evil against a fellow saint can never bring peace in the midst of strife and contention. Neither can rebellion against sound words or counsel resolve problems for one who is self-willed.

Scripture References
Proverbs 11:14, 29; 12:1, 15, 21; 13:18; 15:10
Isaiah 5:20
Romans 12:17-18, 21
I Peter 3:9-10

82. "NO MAN KNOWS EVERYTHING"

Pride and vanity are "blinders" that prevent people from seeing the best God has to offer them. When one boasts of how much he "knows, " you can be assured he's trying to impress others in matters that he's ignorant of. The Bible says, "we are going unto perfection, " but we're not there yet and there's always room for improvement.

Scripture References
Proverbs 10:21; 12:15; 18:7; 24:7
Ecclesiastes 10:11-14
Isaiah 5:21
Romans 12:3, 16
I Corinthians 8:1-3
Philippians 3:12

83. "GOD DON'T NEED US, WE NEED GOD"

Because one has walked with God for a number of years, sometimes complacency sets in, and a saint can be deluded in thinking that's he has "arrived." God in his "permissive" will can allow circumstances to beset such a one to acknowledge that he can do nothing without God.

Scripture References
Job 9:3-22, 32-33; 14:7-14; 23:3-14; 38th chapter
Proverbs 8:33-36
Hebrews 12:5-11

84. "GOD WILL PUT STEEL IN YOUR BACK TO STAND ANYTHING"

The belief that if one comes to God, all his problems are over is not true according to the scriptures. In reality they've just begun and the trials or troubles that one faces can sometimes be grievous. God promised in his word that he would strengthen and build us up to meet life's challenges.

Scripture References
II Chronicles 25:8
Psalms 68:35
Isaiah 40:28-31
St. John 1:12
Acts 1:8

85. "YOU DON'T KNOW WHERE DEATH IS AT"

No one knows what the next day will bring, which is why we who are saved must live for God as if , " it's the last day of our life." Whether we go the grave route, or alive in the rapture, it's essential to be found in the will of God if death seizes us.

Scripture References
Job 14:7-14
Psalms 89:48
Ecclesiastes 3:20
II Corinthians 4:7; 5:1-4
II Timothy 4:8, 18
James 4:14

86. "TAKING A GOOD BUCKET OF MILK AND KICKING IT OVER"

There are some people that don't appreciate the good fortunes that God has blessed them with. They take such things for granted or misuse them for carnal pursuits, soon their lack of responsibility catches up and brings great sorrow and heartache.

Scripture References
Deuteronomy 28:1-9, 15-20
Psalms 107:17
St. Matthew 25:14-30
St. Luke 12:15-21
I Timothy 6:7
Revelation 3:17

87. "RAKE THE WORD TO YOURSELF, AND DON'T USE A SHOVEL"

The word of God is meant to be received into our hearts, so that it can germinate and make us grow in the Lord. We must not cast away the word from us because it condemns us when we're wrong, or insinuate that it's meant for others.

Scripture References
Deuteronomy 6:5-11
Job 23:12
Psalms 119:11
St. Matthew 13:3-23)

88. "THERE'S THREE SIDES TO EVERY STORY, HIS SIDE, HER SIDE, AND THE RIGHT SIDE"

In solving differences between saints, a pastor must be objective and impartial in handling the issues being discussed. Personal feelings for one or the other are left out so that the merits of the case are treated fairly. The problem is solved by the best authority available, the word of God. This is especially true when dealing with married couples, because any leaning toward one against the other due to prejudice tears the relationship apart.

Scripture References
Job 13:10
Proverbs 24:23-25; 28:21
Malachi 2:14-16
II Corinthians 5:18-20
I Timothy 5:21
James 2:4

89. "AN EMPTY WAGON CARRIES A LOT OF NOISE"

There is much formality and pretension in churches today, with people trying to impress others by how well they sing, dance, or testify. Salvation isn't predicated on a outward show of piety, but on the reality of living right for God in a sinful world. Many have deceived themselves in believing that displaying these "acts" of worship makes them "saved." Yet after the service is over, their conduct can be unbecoming for a saint of God.

Scripture References
Psalms 2:1; 127:1-2
Ezekiel 33:31-32
St. Matthew 6:5; 7:21
Romans 14:17
I Corinthians 13:1-3
I Timothy 3:15
II Timothy 3:5

90. "WARNING COMES BEFORE DESTRUCTION"

Throughout the Old Testament, we find numerous situations of God sending his prophets to proclaim warnings to Israel. When they ignored the words of God's servants, punishment was the result. The same holds true today in the church as dismissing the word of warning will likewise bring severe consequences.

Scripture References
Ezekiel 3:17-21; 33:7-16
Acts 20:31
Hebrews 2:1-3; 3:12-13, 18-19; 4:1-2, 11; 6:4-8; 12:25-29

91. "IF I STEPPED ON YOUR TOES, EXCUSE ME, I'LL GET YOUR WHOLE FOOT THE NEXT TIME"

As previously stated, Bishop Tucker's manner of preaching the word was straight and hard. Knowing that it didn't please everyone did not move him to change, because of his conviction to tell the truth. They that love God readily received it and others who did not remained miserable until they humbled themselves and repented

Scripture References
Job 5:17,19
Isaiah 58:1
Jeremiah 23:29
St. Matthew 21:44
I Thessalonians 5:14
II Thessalonians 3:14-15
Titus 2:8-10, 15

92. "PEOPLE WILL USE YOU FOR WHAT THEY CAN GET, THEN DROP YOU LIKE A HOT POTATO"

Jesus spoke one of the signs of these last days as being, "iniquity abounding, and the love of many waxing cold." Sad to say, but there is a spirit of selfishness and deceit being perpetrated among the saints of God. There are those who because of carnality will manipulate and take advantage of the kindness and trust shown to them by fellow saints. Once their ulterior motives are satisfied, they suddenly end the relationship, leaving the trusting saint hurt and wounded. Such persons are insensitive to the feelings of others, and bring shame to a church.

Scripture References
Proverbs 21:6; 22:16
Jeremiah 22:13
Ezekiel 22:12-13
St. Matthew 23:25; 24:10-12
Ephesians 4:19
Titus 1:10-11
II Peter 2:3,18
Jude16

93. "GIVE A FOOL ENOUGH ROPE, AND HE'LL HANG HIMSELF"

People who are arrogant and rebellious, having never received discipline, eventually fall victims to their own contrary ways. They may enjoy the "pleasures of sin for a season, " but then the reaping of what they've sown will come to pass.

Scripture References
Proverbs 2:11-15; 4:19; 25:28; 26:11-12; 28:13-14; 29:1

94. "THERE'S THE DOOR THAT THE CARPENTER HUNG, IT SWINGS BOTH WAYS"

Similar to Nos. 65 and 71, Bishop Tucker's no-nonsense approach to ministering the word would either draw or drive one away from the church. He was plain concerning the fact that whether a saint comes or goes, the "Word" remains the same.

Scripture References
II Corinthians 4:1-5
Philippians 1:17
II Timothy 4:1-7

95. "WHAT PEOPLE DON'T KNOW, WON'T HURT THEM"

There are some things that are best left unsaid for fear of causing hurt to an individual. Even that which is true can be harmful if given at the wrong time. Care and consideration should be exercised on behalf of any saint of God. Only one who truly loves a fellow saint would use discretion in the handling of information he deems necessary or not.

Scripture References
Proverbs 12:23; 13:16; 14:15; 22:3
Amos 5:13
Ephesians 5:12

96. "DON'T GO TO DUMBSVILLE"

Usually when a person becomes dishonest, he tends to feign ignorance of what he said or did when confronted. Not wanting to take responsibility for his actions, he attempts to divert attention from himself and mislead others. Such actions only delay the inevitable of having to "face up" to his wrongs.

Scripture References
Psalms 52:3; 92:6
Proverbs 28:13
Isaiah 29:15
Jeremiah 4:22; 5; 4
Zechariah 7:12
St. Matthew 13:15
St. John 3:20
Romans 1:28; 10:3
Ephesians 5:11

97. "PEOPLE ARE CROOKS, AND COME FROM CROOKS"

This is not a personal indictment from Bishop Tucker, but a universal fact as expressed by the word of God concerning unregenerate mankind. The whole world has been under the curse of sin since Adam's disobedience, and until man comes to repentance, his thoughts and actions shall always be in rebellion against God.

Scripture References
Genesis 6:5
I Samuel 15:23
Job 5:2; 9:20; 15:16
Psalms 51:5; 66:18
Ezekiel 18:20
St. Matthew 7:21-23
Romans 5:12-21; 6:23

98. "BEWARE OF THE SPIRITUAL HOBO"

Though Jesus speaks in the scriptures about the "poor you'll have with you always, " he did not have in mind the character that preys on the generosity of the saints. These "scavengers" with their tales of woe and misfortune take advantage of the kindness shown unto them. They make a living "hitting" on folks for food, money and clothes then give false promises of paying back what they owe. Once their scam is discovered they quickly leave and go to another church to practice their craft.

Scripture References
Job 5:12-13; 15:2-5
Psalms 37:21; 125:5
Proverbs 6:9-15; 21:6, 17; 28:19

99. "STAY OUT OF THE CLIQUES"

Cliques are defined as a small exclusive group of people that operates on a certain agenda in the church. Some are friendly and harmless, but the majority tends to be run diversely from the rest of the church. They are the carnal segment of a church whose activities, if not addressed by the Pastor, can wreak havoc in the church. Such persons can adversely affect others from sincerely walking with God, and discourage them to do what is right and proper as a saint.

Scripture References
Exodus 23:2
Psalms 1:1
Proverbs 1:10-19; 4:14; 24:1
I Corinthians 1:10-15; 3:1-5; 5:11
II Corinthians 6:14
Ephesians 5:11
II Thessalonians 3:6

100. "THE DARKEST HOUR IS JUST BEFORE THE DAWN"

When going through grievous trials, the situations can be such that there seems to be no way out. Bishop Tucker reminded us that God is always there to rescue us in the nick of time, and give us the victory over what appeared to be impossible.

Scripture References
Exodus 14:13-14
Psalms 37:34-40
Proverbs 4:18
Isaiah 9:2; 40:29-31; 41:10; 58:8-12
St. John 8:12
II Corinthians 12:7-10
I John 3:3

101. "DON'T LET ANYONE GET SOMETHING ON YOU THAT HE WOULD WASH YOUR FACE WITH LATER"

One should carefully choose his confidants. When differences of opinions occur, one will betray your trust and try to ruin your reputation.

Scripture References
Psalm 31:13; 101:5
Proverbs 10:18; 11:9; 16:28; 26:19-26
James 4:11
I Peter 2:1

102. "PEOPLE WILL GIVE YOU ADVICE THAT THEY WON'T USE THEMSELVES"

Beware of the know-it-all who has life's answers for your problems and will not apply their advice to their own situation. Jesus said, "you shall know them by their fruit." This is the measuring stick that determines the value of a man's word.

Scripture References
Job 11:2
Proverbs 10:19; 14:23; 29:11
Ecclesiastes 10:11-13
Titus 1:10

103. "YOU DON'T KNOW NOBODY UNTIL YOU HAVE DEALINGS WITH THEM"

"Dealings" is another way of stating interactions. A person we interact with on a daily basis, we don't know them as well as we think we do. Circumstances will arise that reveal a side of a person that you didn't anticipate and can be unpleasant to handle.

Scripture References
Proverbs 3:30; 17:14; 25:8
Acts 15:36-40;
Philippians 2:3
II Timothy 2:14, 24-25
Hebrews 13:1-2

104. "BLESSED IS THE PREACHER WHO CAN TESTIFY WITHOUT PREACHING"

This saying refers to a praise service in which a member who happens to be a minister uses such time as a forum to express himself by preaching rather than testifying of the goodness of God as others. He often dominates a service to satisfy what is called by some as the "preacher's itch." They fail to see that there's an appointed time for such things, and discipline should be exercised on one's conduct in consideration to others.

Scripture References
Proverbs 17:27; 25:11
Ecclesiastes 10:12
Isaiah 50:4
Romans 12:6-10

I Corinthians 14:20, 26, 29-33, 40
James 3:2

105. "PEOPLE WHO TALK TOO MUCH WILL EVENTUALLY START LYING"

When people talk out of control, harmless banter can soon turn into false statements creating chaos and confusion in the church. Such activities must be avoided at all costs.

Scripture References
Job 9:20
Psalms 55:21; 119:163
Proverbs 6:16-17; 10:14; 13:5; 19:5, 9; 26:28
Jeremiah 7:4
Ephesians 4:25
Colossians 3:9
I Timothy 4:2
Revelation 22:15

106. "IF YOU PLAY ME FOR A FOOL, YOU'LL LOSE YOUR MONEY"

A pastor's job allows him the experience of dealing with people on a wide range. Still you have those who will deceive an intention with flattery and acts of charity. A wise pastor has such a spirit of discernment that he will not act impulsively, but wait out the situation to discern the ulterior motives of a person. Once the offender's actions are known, there is shame and embarrassment to him.

Scripture References
Psalm 52:4; 101:7
Proverbs 12:20, 27:6
Jeremiah 9:17

St. Luke 6:26
Ephesians 4:14-15
Titus 1:10-11

107. "YOU HAVE TO WEAR THIS WORLD LIKE A LOOSE GARMENT"

The scriptures tell us that "we are in the world, but not of the world" and as a saint, we cannot live close to the world in its carnal attitudes and lifestyles. We must always endeavor to live a clean and separate life from the negative ways of this present evil world.

Scripture References
St. John 15:18-21; 17:14-18
Acts 4:13
Romans 13:11-14
II Corinthians 6:14-18; 7:1
Philippians 2:15
I Peter 2:9

108. "DECEPTIVE PEOPLE WILL TELL YOU TO MEET THEM DOWN ON BROAD STREET, BUT YOU'LL FIND THEM ON RIDGE AVENUE"

This saying of Bishop Tucker's denotes the dishonesty of persons who try to divert one's attention from what they really mean through double-talk and chicanery. Broad Street and Ridge Avenue are known Philadelphia streets used as metaphors to describe such misleading actions.

Scripture References
Leviticus 19:13
Psalm 119:104; 120:3
Proverbs 12:17; 17:4

I Timothy 3:8
James 1:8; 4:8

109. "SIN STINKS IN GOD'S NOSTRILS"

Sin as illustrated in the Bible is a violation and transgression of God's holy word, and is indeed a thing that carries a foul stench before Him. Man's depraved nature as a result of sin will continually keep many apart from God, until they come to believe and obey the Gospel.

Scripture References
Psalm 38:1-5
Proverbs 28:13
Isaiah 59:1-3
Jeremiah 2:22; 6:20-21
Amos 5:21

110. "GOD WILL SLAP THE TASTE OUT OF YOUR MOUTH, IF YOU CONTINUE TO BE DISOBEDIENT"

A person who refuses to take heed to God's word and warning will in time suffer the consequences of his actions. Though God is gracious and merciful, even he will set limits on tolerating one's wickedness.

Scripture References
Deuteronomy 28:15-22
I Samuel 15:16-29
Proverbs 1:22-32; 6:12-19
Isaiah 1:18-20

111. "ALL EXCUSES ARE NAILED TO THE CROSS"

When a person has been delivered from the bondage of sin, he remembers the helplessness of living such a life and appreciates the new life in Christ. At times he makes excuses to justify his actions, therefore becoming weak and complacent. He forgets that Christ's work at Calvary has enabled him to receive the power to triumph over such obstacles.

Scripture References
St. John 1:12
Acts 1:8
Romans 13:14
I Corinthians 1:17-18; 15:12-22
II Corinthians 12:9-10
Ephesians 2:13-16
Colossians 1:20-22; 2:14
II Timothy 1:7

112. "PEOPLE WILL THROW CROWBARS AND BRICKBATS AT YOU"

The Apostle Paul said in II Timothy 3:12, "all that will live godly in Christ Jesus shall suffer persecution." Not only shall opposition come from the world, but also in the church from those who envy your sincere walk with Jesus. The Apostle speaks of these last days of persons being traitors and despisers of those that are good, and would slander the good name of any saint.

Scripture References
Psalm 37:9
Proverbs 11:12; 14:21

St. Luke 10:16
Ephesians 4:32
Romans 2:9
Galatians 5:12
Colossians 3:5-10
II Thessalonians 1:4-10
Hebrews 10:26-31

113. "SOME FOLKS WILL TAKE THE BENEFIT, AND LEAVE YOU WITH THE DOUBT"

Beware of the person who is getting the better of a relationship by being on the receiving end the majority of the time, and makes excuses when it's their turn to reciprocate. They are selfish and only want to take advantage of your kindness to them. Their interest in you will wane once you cease to give in to them, and the true nature of their self is revealed.

Scripture References
Proverbs 3:27-31; 23:6-8; 26:24-26
Jeremiah 9:5; 17:9; 22:13
II Peter 2:13-14

114. "JESUS IS THE GREATEST ROOT WORKER"

Bishop Tucker's description of Jesus here is not of one working witchcraft, but of the Bible's speaking of Him as the "Root of Jesse and the offspring of David." He's called also in Isaiah as the "Branch", and in the Gospel of John as the "True Vine." In reference to these symbolic descriptions of Jesus, Bishop Tucker would say that Jesus' purpose was to "root" us out of sin.

Scripture References
Isaiah 11:1-5; 61:1-3
Zechariah 6:12-15
St. John 15:1-6
Romans 11:16-25
I Corinthians 3:6-11
Revelation 22:16

115. "MONEY DOES FUNNY THINGS TO PEOPLE"

Though the Bible speaks of money as "answering all things" as found in Ecclesiastes 10:19, the flip side of it says that "the love of money is the root of all evil" as given in I Timothy 6:10. There are some who have a weakness for money and go to such lengths to betray or manipulate friends in order to obtain it. Without it, they are easy to get along with until an opportunity to have money come their way, and a sudden change in character takes place in them.

Scripture References
Psalms 15:5; 62:10
Proverbs 11:4, 28; 13:7; 27:24; 28:20
Ecclesiastes 5:10-16
Jeremiah 17:11
St. Mark 10:23
I Timothy 6:17
James 5:2
Revelation 3:17

116. "YOU CAN CATCH MORE FLIES WITH HONEY, THAN YOU CAN WITH VINEGAR"

As saints of God, we are required to be witnesses to an unsaved world. However, presenting Christ to others can be rendered ineffective if given with a sour disposition or in a critical manner. A true soul winner can win people to Christ in the way He demonstrated, with loving compassion and consideration to all people.

Scripture References
Proverbs 11:30
St. Matthew 9:36
Ephesians 4:32
Colossians 3:12
I Corinthians 9:18-23
II Peter 1:7-9

117. "A ROLLING STONE GATHERS NO MOSS"

When Jesus gave the parable concerning the sower who sowed seeds in the field, he spoke of some seeds falling upon stony places that had little ground underneath. Because it had no depth, they were scorched by the sun and withered. There are people who run from church to church due to restlessness and instability, never stay long enough to mature in God through the word. Like the parable they can't cope with problems that arise in their lives and are soon departed to another place trying to find solace and comfort.

Scripture References
Job 11:14-15
Psalms 27:14; 37:34

Proverbs 14:29
Ecclesiastes 5:2
Lamentations 3:25
St. Matthew 13:3-23
I Corinthians 15:58
James 1:8; 4:8
II Peter 2:14; 3:16-18
I John 2:19; 4:18
Jude 3-4, 12-13

118. "WHEN YOU'RE PRAYING FOR PATIENCE, YOU'RE ASKING FOR TROUBLE"

Patience is defined as calm endurance, and often the saint of God has difficulty exercising such an attribute when hard times occur. The Bible tells us that going through adversity is how we learn to be patient, and it builds in us godly character. God in His permissive will allows troublesome situations in our lives so that we gain the ability to overcome them and become mature believers for the experience.

Scripture References
Job 14:1, 7-14
Psalms 27:13-14, 37:7, 40:1
Isaiah 40:29-31
St. Luke 21:19
Romans 5:3-5; 12:12
Hebrews 10:36
James 1:2-4; 5:7

119. "YOU DON'T HAVE TO BELIEVE WHAT I'M TEACHING; THAT'S YOUR GOD-GIVEN RIGHT"

Whenever Bishop Tucker preached our taught the word of God, he could discern when everyone wasn't receiving the word. As he explained to the people, it was their choice to accept the word or not, being creatures with the ability to exercise free will. He warned them of the consequences they must face for making such a decision concerning the word of God.

Scripture References
Deuteronomy 30:19
Joshua 24:15
I Kings 18:21-39
Psalms 25:12
St. John 6:53-68; 8:24; 12:47-48
Romans 10:14-17; 14:23
Hebrews 3:6-13; 4:1-6; 11:1-6
James 1:22

120. "THE BEST THING THAT PEOPLE CAN SAY ABOUT YOU SOMETIMES IS THE WORST"

Though any person would love to be well spoken of by his or her peers, not everyone will speak complimentary of you. Even in the church, there will be some that would criticize and defame your character for being a child of God. Although being human, we feel the pain and hurts of such verbal attacks, remember that Jesus, our example, endured the slurs hurled by those who opposed Him.

Scripture References
Psalm 31:13-18; 101:2-6
Proverbs 10:18; 11:9
Jeremiah 9:4-6
St. Matthew 5:11-12; 9:32-34; 11:18-19; 27:63
St. Mark 3:20-21
St. Luke 6:26
St. John 7:20, 9:16; 10:19-21
I Peter 2:12; 4:3-4

121. "WHEN GOD WITHHOLDS A THING FROM YOU, IT'S BECAUSE HE HAS SOMETHING BETTER IN STORE FOR YOU"

God, in His divine providence, knows our hearts and what's best for us. Sometimes when making a request to God, disappointment sets in when we don't receive what we asked of Him. He may hold back due to our immaturity to handle what is given to us or a circumstance that He foresees as detrimental to our spiritual lives. Once God pours out His blessing upon us, we learn that what we have received from Him far exceeds our initial expectation.

Scripture References
Job 23:1-10, 13-14; 42:10-13
II Samuel 12:15-16, 23-24
Psalms 13th chapter
St. Matthew 5:45; 6:31-33
St. Luke 11:5-13; 18:1-8
Acts 17:24-28
Romans 8:24-28
II Corinthians 12:8-9
Ephesians 1:18-19
James 1:6-7, 17

122. "CUTTING OFF YOUR NOSE IN SPITE OF YOUR FACE"

Neither pride or selfishness would improve one's character; as the saying implies, mutilating one's face will not enhance beauty in the eye of the beholder. Do not make a situation worse with the intent on hurting another, when in fact, you made the situation worse.

Scripture References
Proverbs 11:22; 31:30
Psalms 149:4
St. Matthew 23:12, 28
Romans 12:3
Galatians 6:3
James 1:22-27; 4:6

123. "WHAT GOD HAS FOR YOU, YOU'RE GOING TO GET IT, AND WHAT'S NOT FOR YOU, THEN YOU WON'T GET IT"

One can rest assured that trusting God on His promises, He will, by His divine Word, bring it to pass. His blessing will fulfill every believer's need. On the flip side, we can be certain that if it's not God's will for one to receive what he asked, no pleading or begging will change the situation.

Scripture References
Psalm 37:3-7
Proverbs 1:22-31; 3:5-6, 9-10, 33-36
Isaiah 59:2
St. Matthew 6:31-33; 7:7-11
St. Luke 6:38
James 1:6-8; 4:1-3

124. "ALL THAT GLITTERS IS NOT GOLD"

Beware of persons whose character comes across as being grand, who sprouts high-sounding words that excite others. They love to be in the forefront of every activity in church, but behind their veneer of godliness lies no substance of true spirituality, only deceit.

Scripture References
Romans 16:17-18
I Corinthians 2:1-8
II Peter 2nd chapter
Jude 4,11-13,16

125. "I WANT TO LIVE AS LONG AS I CAN, AND DIE WHEN I HAVE TO"

These words spoken by Bishop Tucker proved to be a fitting epitaph for one who had lived a full life serving God and His people. Though he stated it in a humorous manner, it revealed the reality of facing his mortality. He had concerns and fears about death as anyone would under such circumstances, and spoke of death as being a "monster." Despite his sickness, he continued to give of himself to the church until he could go no further. In the end, he faced death like a man and left this earthly sphere to be with the Lord, leaving a legacy for others to follow. I salute him.

Scripture References
Job 14:14; 19:25-27
Psalm 89:48
St. John 9:4
II Corinthians 5:1-8
II Timothy 4:6-8

126. "DON'T RUN TO EVERY DOG AND CAT FIGHT"

It's one thing to be confronted with unpleasant situations that are not of your own doing, but to be purposely involved in arguing or debating with others can be unwise and cause repercussions that are difficult to overcome. Some situations are better avoided than trying to win an argument at any cost.

Scripture References
Proverbs 3:30; 13:16; 17:14; 20:3; 25:8; 26:17
Philippians 2: 3
2nd Timothy 2:14, 24
James 3:14

127. "THE WORD TO SOME PEOPLE IS LIKE WATER OFF A DUCK'S BACK"

People who become lax in the faith will grow complacent and unconcerned about spiritual matters. Hearing the word of God holds no place in their hearts when they become insensitive and callous in attitude towards God.
Scripture References
Psalms 92:6
Isaiah 6:10
Jcromiah 6:10
Ezekiel 12:2
Micah 4:12
St. John 8:43
Acts 28:27
Hebrews 4:1-2; 5:11-14

128. "THERE'S A DEAD CAT ON THE LINE SOMEWHERE"

When disruption occurs creating problems where there was once harmony among church members, the cause may not appear immediately but in time suspicions become apparent as the actions of the guilty party are made manifest and exposed for all to see.

Scripture References
Psalms 83:3; 101:7
Proverbs 6:19; 12:22; 19:19; 26:21-28; 28:12-13
Matthew 10:26
1st Corinthians 4:5
2nd Corinthians 4:2

129. "LETTING THE CAT OUT OF THE BAG"

Exercising discretion in the keeping of information for appropriate times is essential in nurturing trust of relationships between believers. Hastily revealing things prematurely without regard to the nature of the matter can only bring chaos and confusion among the saints.

Scripture References
Psalms 112:5
Proverbs 2:11; 11:13; 15:14; 18:7,13; 19:11; 26:11

130. "SHOTGUN CONFESSIONS"

There's no real honor in confessing one's "wrongs" as a result of being coerced or "shamed" into admitting your sins. We are to voluntarily confess our faults on the conviction and repentance of our hearts towards God.

Scripture References
Numbers 32:23
Joshua 7: 19-26
2nd Samuel 12: 1-14
Job 20:27
Proverbs 26:26
Ecclesiastes 12:14

131. "BECAUSE OF WHO I AM AND WHAT I REPRESENT"

The Apostle Paul stated in the book of Romans that one ought not to think of himself more highly than he ought to think, but to think soberly. It's particularly sad when one starts humbly walking with God but in time becomes arrogant when assuming leadership positions in church. His vain attitude alienates others and stirs up contentions as well.

Scripture References
2nd Chronicles 26:16
Job 33:9
Psalms 73: 6
Proverbs 6: 17; 11:2; 21: 4
Isaiah 5: 21
Daniel 4:30-32; 5: 17-23
Luke 18: 11
Romans 12:3
1st Corinthians 4:18

132. "IT'S JUST NICE TO BE NICE"

The Christian life is exemplified by Jesus' words, "then will men know that you are my disciples for the love you have one to another". Doing well for a fellow believer must be a staple of daily life so that the blessings from God's word can enrich one's life to spiritual maturity. The world can only see Jesus reflected through our lives.

Scripture References
Matthew 12:46-50
John 13: 34-35
Romans 12:10
1st Corinthians 13:4
Galatians 6: 10
Ephesians 4:32
Colossians 3:12
2nd Peter 1:5-8

133. "THE CHURCH WASN'T MADE FOR GOOD PEOPLE"

Contrary to popular belief, a church is not intended for the morally upright and pious among us, but rather the spiritually sick and impoverished. It is a place where men can be delivered from the ravages of sin, be renewed to become witnesses of the life-changing power of God. Here is where people learn how to live the way God desires.

Scripture References
Job 15: 14-16
Psalms 14:1-3
Isaiah   1:5-6; 64: 6
Jeremiah 17: 9-10
Matthew 5: 20; 9: 10-13; 18: 3
Luke 4:18; 13: 1-3
Romans 3: 23; 5:6-8, 14-22
1st John 1: 8-10

134. "PEOPLE TESTIFY IN FIVE MINUTES WHAT THEY CAN'T LIVE IN FIVE YEARS"

Too often in praise and worship services there are those who for the purpose of impressing others will wax eloquent about what the Lord has done in their lives. Closer scrutiny of the things they proclaim will find that often how they live comes up short in comparison to what is said. We should be careful how we testify in church for God knows what is in our hearts, and statements that are untrue can prove in time to be our undoing.

Scripture References
Job 15:34
Psalms 1:1,5; 51: 16-17
Proverbs 12:5; 20:6; 23: 7; 26:25; 30:12
Ecclesiastes 5:1
Isaiah 1: 11-20
Matthew 15:7-9; 23:14,28
Luke 6: 46
Romans 16: 17-18
1st Timothy 4: 1-2
2nd Timothy 3:5
Titus 1: 16

135. "YOU SAID IT, THESE ARE YOUR WORDS"

Jesus once said, "by your words you are justified and by your words you are condemned". Great care should be taken when making promises to someone on the premise that you will follow up on what you say. Bishop Tucker stated that people conveniently forget to fulfill what they agreed to others and try to back out with flimsy excuses when reminded. It shows dishonesty in the one who made such promises.

Scripture References
Job 9:20; 11:2-6; 15:3-6
Psalms 34:13
Proverbs 10:19; 14:23; 29:11
Ecclesiastes 10:12-14
Matthew 5:37; 12:35-37
Colossians 4:6
Titus 2: 8
James 3:2

136. "YOU CAN ACT A LIE AS WELL AS TELL ONE"

Lying not only can be expressed vocally, but also one's actions can reveal the wrong intentions contrary to his words.

Scripture References
Job 5:12-13
Psalms 10:2-7; 28:3; 38:12; 101:7
Proverbs 10:23; 12:5; 24:8, 16; 28:14
2nd Corinthians 11:13; 12:26
Colossians 2:8

137. "IF YOU DIE LOST HAVING KNOWN GOD, YOU OUGHT TO BURN WELL"

Living beneath one's privilege after knowing God's word can prove detrimental to the careless believer. Many of Jesus' parables dealt with the accountability of stewards and the blessings or punishment rendered to them according to their conduct. The scriptures tell us that it is better not to have known the ways of God than to decide to walk away from him.

Scripture References
Nehemiah 9:35
Ezekiel 33:7-13, 18-19
Matthew 7: 26-27
Luke 11:26; 12:47
John 6: 63-66
Romans 1: 18-25, 32
Hebrews 3:12-14,17-19; 4:1-2, 11
James 4:17
2nd Peter 2:1-4, 9, 15-22
Revelations 21:8; 22:18-19

138. "THERE'S ONE THING CERTAIN AND TWO THINGS SURE"

In a world where fads and fashions come and go and secular philosophies tell us there's no absolutes but truth is only relative, God's word says otherwise. The immutability of God's divine will and authority makes plain that man's destiny is determined and inevitable despite man's unbelief.

Scripture References
Deuteronomy 32:40
Job 14:1, 5, 7-14; 15: 14-16
Psalms 102: 25-26
Malachi 3: 6
Acts 17:24-27, 31
Romans 11:33
Galatians 6:7-8
Hebrews 6: 17-18; 9:27; 13:8
James 1:17

139. "WHEN BIG BELLS TOLL IN ZION, LITTLE BELLS KEEP QUIET"

In a time when lack of respect is being displayed towards church leaders, the Bible makes clear the repercussions against any that would behave in such manner. Examples in both the Old and New Testaments show the blessings received by those who honor leadership and the punishment suffered by the rebellious.

Scripture References
Numbers 12th chapter
Proverbs 13:18; 22:4; 29:23
Isaiah 50:10
Acts 5:1-11
Romans 13:1-7
1st Thessalonians 5:12-13
1st Timothy 5:17-19
Hebrews 13:7, 17
1st Peter 5:5

140. "SOME PEOPLE CRY EVEN WHEN THEY HAVE A LOAF OF BREAD UNDER THEIR ARM"

We should always be thankful for what God has provided for us, and content with whatever we receive in this life. Sadly, there are those who can never have enough or complain even though they possess all they need.

Scripture References
Exodus 15:23-25; 16:2-20
Proverbs 15:16; 19:3
1st Corinthians 10:10
Philippians 2:14; 4:11

1st Timothy 6:6-8
Hebrews 13:5

141. "PEW PASTORS"

Though the pastor is the spiritual leader of the church and responsible for the souls under his watch, there are some among the congregation who think they can counsel fellow members from where they sit. Such persons are disruptive and usually give advice that is harmful to a fellow saint. They are stumblingblocks who wield great influence over others and prevent them from following proper guidelines in church.

Scripture References
Proverbs 17:27
Matthew 5:37
Romans 16:17-18
Ephesians 4:14-15, 22-25, 29-32
1st Timothy 1:19-20; 4:1-2,7; 5:12-13; 6:3-5
2nd Timothy 2:14-19, 23-26; 3:1-9; 4:3-4
2nd Peter 2:1-3, 10-14
3rd John .9-11

142. "THE THREE BOOKS THAT RUN THE CHURCH"

Bishop Tucker taught the three books that run the church was the good book, which is the Bible, our spiritual foundation through the word of God. Next, is the hymnbook that provides many of the songs of praise and the pocketbook, which are our contributions in the support of the church.

Scripture References
Deuteronomy 16:17
Psalms 33:3; 40:3; 149:1
Proverbs 3:9
Malachi 3:10

John 6:63, 68; 14:6
Luke 6:38; 11:41
Romans 10:14-17
2nd Corinthians 4:1-6
Ephesians 2:20-22
Colossians 3:16

143. "TELL THE TRUTH AND SHAME THE DEVIL"

When we commit a wrong, sometimes the guilt of what we've done makes it difficult to confess. Failure in confessing our sins only gives the enemy power over us and prevents the blessing of God in our lives. By confessing them this breaks the hold of Satan and makes us victorious to continue enjoying our freedom in Christ.

Scripture References
2nd Samuel 24:10-14
Ezra 10:11-14
Psalms 41:4; 51st chapter
Proverbs 28:13
Jeremiah 3:13
2nd Corinthians 7:1
2nd Timothy 2:21
James 4:8
1st John 1:7-9

144. "PRAYER WILL KEEP YOU FIT FOR SERVICE"

As water and food are essential in maintaining our lives daily, prayer holds the same significance in our spiritual walk. The Bible is full of scriptures giving examples of the power of prayer in the lives of them that serve God. Daily communicating with God will enable the believer to grow and mature in becoming effective in ministry.

Scripture References
Psalms 4:3; 34:15-19; 40:1
Isaiah 56:7
Matthew 7:7
Luke 18:1; 21:36
John 16:24
Romans 8:26-27
Ephesians 6:18
1st Thessalonians 5:17
James 5:13, 16
1st John 3:22

145. "DON'T WALK BOW-LEGGED OR KNOCK-KNEED"

Our walk with God is to be traveled as a straight path that leads to the eternal glory promised us. However, when one strays from the way he can become spiritually sick and fall by the wayside.

Scripture References
Genesis 17:1
Psalms 26:11; 84; 11
Proverbs 13:20; 28:26
Isaiah 40:31
Micah 6:8
Matthew 18:8
Romans 13:13; 14:15

Colossians 2:6
2nd Peter 3:3
1st John 2:11

146. "THE DEVIL WILL GET YOU IN A LOT OF TROUBLE, BUT WON'T GET YOU OUT OF IT"

Living in the flesh involves following the carnal and worldly appetites prevalent today. Here is where Satan, who is described by Apostle Paul as the "God of this world" imposes his influence throughout our society. To follow his path may give one pleasure, but soon can become a nightmare leaving one to suffer the consequences of his actions.

Scripture References
Genesis 3:1-15
Joshua 7:20-26
Judges 16:4-21
1st Kings 11:1-4
Proverbs 13:15
Luke 11:23:26
John 8:44
2nd Corinthians 12:20-21
Galatians 3:1-4
Ephesians 4:26-27; 5:5-7
2nd Timothy 2:22-26
James 4:7

147. "THERE'S NOTHING WORSE THAN A HEARTACHE"

We can endure the physical pain of illness or mishaps that befalls us on occasions. Our wounds will heal and the pain subsides in time, but to receive spiritual hurts inflicted on us by others can indeed be excruciating. Betrayal of trust by a fellow member in church is particularly painful when the offender refuses to reconcile or acknowledge his wrong. Only God can relieve the victim of such hurt and bring deliverance in due time.

Scripture References
Psalms 31:9, 12-13; 34:18-19; 42:5-6; 147:3
Proverbs 12:25; 15:13; 17:22; 18:14
Jeremiah 23:9
Zechariah 13:6
Matthew 23:37-39
John 1:10-11
Romans 15:4
2nd Corinthians 1:3-4

148. "GOD HAS A WAY THAT'S MIGHTY SWEET"

Following the path of God can be an exhilarating experience as we receive the abundance of blessings that he promised in his word. His divine love overshadows us and provides comfort even in the midst of storms in our lives. From our experiences we gain understanding and insight to his will and purpose for bringing us to growth and maturity. Our future is secure and hope is enlivened by the prospect of what he has in store for us.

Scripture References
Psalms 19:7-10; 23.6; 34:8; 145:9
Isaiah 35:8-10; 40:9-14, 28-31; 46:10; 55:9
Daniel 2:19-22
John 3:8
Romans 11:33
1st Corinthians 1:25-31; 2:6-12; 15:38-58
Ephesians 1:3-14, 17-23; 2:4-7, 18-22
Philippians 2:5-11

Colossians 1:13-22
1ˢᵗ Thessalonians 4:13-18

149. "GOD'LL KEEP YOU IF YOU WANT TO BE KEPT"

The Holy Ghost was given to believers as a guide and helper to live victoriously in today's troubled world. How effective we become in our service to God depends on our desire to yield daily to his will. If we fall back to our carnal ways this will lead to a return to our sinful past and render us weak and futile.

Scripture References
Genesis 28:11-17
Deuteronomy 33:27
Psalms 22:28-30; 25:20-21; 121:5
Proverbs 4:23
John 14:15; 17:11, 15
Romans 6:11-18; 7:21-25
1ˢᵗ Peter 1:5
Jude 21, 23

150. "RIGHT IS RIGHT AND WRONG IS WRONG"

This is a time where society's morals have descended to an all-time low and great care is given to being politically correct so as not to offend anyone. Right and wrong have blended into such a blur that there is no guideline or principle to determine what's proper or not. Sadly, this spirit has crept into the church and adversely affected many. The Church must take the initiative to return to those Biblical standards that made her great and steer society's moral compass in the right direction.

Scripture References
Deuteronomy 28:1-22
Job 15:14
Psalms 1:6; 34:17; 37:17
Proverbs 10:28-30; 14:34; 15:29
Isaiah 5:20-24
Jeremiah 17:9-10
Matthew 15:1-20
Romans 6:1-2, 19-23; 13:9-14
Ephesians 2:1-3; 4:17-19, 22-25
Hebrews 10:26-31
James 3:14-18; 4:1-6
Revelations 22:11

151. "DON'T EAT OFF OF EVERY-BODY'S TABLE"

It is essential for the child of God to eat the right and proper spiritual food to mature and grow in his walk with God. Avoiding false doctrines and philosophies of men is key to the conscientious believer in maintaining good health and efficiency in service.

Scripture References
Job 23:12
Proverbs 7:1-3
Isaiah 28: 7-13
Daniel 1: 5-16
Malachi 1: 6-8
Matthew 16: 5-12
Luke 12: 1-2
1st Corinthians 10:20-23
Ephesians 5: 11-13
Colossians 2:8
2nd Peter 2: 12-15

152. "FOLKS WON'T GIVE YOU CREDIT FOR GOING ALONG WITH THEIR WRONGDOING"

Cavorting with others in mischief doesn't necessarily win favor for the one who thinks it will gain him acceptance. This is particularly true of those who hold responsible positions in church. They fail to see that condoning the wrongs of others only make them lose respect in the eyes of the offending party. When dire consequences overwhelm those who commit unlawful acts the blame is usually place at the hands of leaders who consented to it in the first place.

Scripture References
Exodus 23:2
Deuteronomy 13: 1-8
1st Kings 13: 7-30
Job 13:9-10
Psalms 1:1
Proverbs 1:10-19; 4:14-17; 11:9; 16:29; 22:24-25; 23:6-7; 28:10
Jeremiah 9:4
Matthew 27:3-5
1st Corinthians 5:9-11
1st Timothy 5:22
2nd Timothy 3:2
Hebrews 12:16-17
James 4:1-6
2nd Peter 2:1-3, 10-12

153. "WE'RE MERCY'S CHILDREN"

The Bible speaks eloquently of the greatness of God's mercy extended towards them that believe in him. His divine love and grace is received not because we're good or earned it through our works but the sacrifice of Jesus on Calvary made it possible. His blood justifies us and makes God's righteousness accessible to all.

Scripture References
Psalms 23:7; 25:7,10; 85:10; 100:5; 103:13
Micah 6:8
Matthew 5:7
Luke 6:36
Romans 9:16; 11:30-31
2nd Corinthians 4:1-2
Ephesians 2:1-7
Titus 3:5
1st Peter 1:3; 2:9-10

154. "I KNOW WHAT YOU CAN DO, WILL DO AND WON'T DO"

As the shepherd of the flock, the pastor must know his sheep in order to provide the spiritual food that will keep them nourished and healthy. He is to be vested with keen insight and discernment to understand the condition of the flock as well as to protect them from predators who would consume them. Also, he must learn to utilize the talents of the group to best advantage for a sufficient ministry and minimize the weaknesses.

Scripture References
Isaiah 62:6-7
Jeremiah 3:15; 6:3; 23:4
Ezekiel 34:12-15
Acts 20:28
2nd Timothy 2:25
Hebrews 13:17
1st Peter 5:1-2

155. "THE ROOM IS BIG ENOUGH FOR EVERYBODY TO HAVE A SEAT"

The Apostle Paul speaks of the Church as an analogy of the human body consisting of many members with different functions and operations. In the church, members may have various offices and responsibilities but the end result is the nurturing and continuity of a growing church. There's no room for big egos or small ones only unity and equality in the edifying of God's people.

Scripture References
Matthew 20:20-28; 23:10-12
John 15:13-15, 20; 17:20-23
Acts 1:13-15; 2:1, 42-46
Romans 12:5
1st Corinthians 1:10; 10:16-17; 12:4-27; 14:40
Ephesians 4:1-13
Philippians 1:27
1st Peter 3:8

156. "...AS HE BOWED HIS HEAD BETWEEN THE LOCKS OF HIS SHOULDERS"

This was a descriptive phrase used by Bishop Tucker to illustrate the last moments of Jesus dying on the cross at Calvary. After uttering his last words, "Into thine hands I commit my spirit," Jesus died. To the mockers and skeptics that surrounded the bloody site at Calvary, they thought it was the end when in reality it was only the beginning.

Scripture References
Matthew 27:45-53, 62-66; 28: 11-15
Mark 15:29-38

Luke 23:39-46
John 19:17-27
Acts 2:14, 22-36; 5:29-32
Romans 5:12-21
1st Corinthians 15th chapter
Philippians 2:5-11
Colossians 1:12-22
Hebrews 2:9-18; 9th chapter

157. "GOD DON'T BLESS OVER NO MESS"

Once a person comes to the knowledge of the truth and receives salvation, he is required to follow the principles of righteousness. To fall back to a carnal and worldly state and still endeavor to live a Christian life is fruitless. Living carelessly and with pretense will not bring God's blessings in the life of him who walks contrary to sound doctrine.

Scripture References
2nd Kings 17:33
Job 8:13; 13:16; 20:5; 27:8
Matthew 23:28
Luke 16:13
1st Corinthians 10:21
Galatians 5:16-26
Ephesians 4:14, 17-27; 5:3-18
Hebrews 13:9
James 1:6-8; 3:17; 4:8

158. "IT'S EVERY MAN FOR HIMSELF AND GOD FOR US ALL"

It is essential to everyone that desires to come to God to make the decision based on the exercising of one's own free will and not of another. Though we are incorporated into the Church as baptized believers in the body of Christ, as individuals there is personal accountability required in our relationships with God.

Scripture References
Deuteronomy 30:15
Joshua 24:14-15
1st Kings 18:21
Ecclesiastes 12:13-14
Isaiah 45:22; 55:1
Ezekiel 3:18; 33:9
Joel 3:14
John 8:24
Acts 4:12
2nd Corinthians 13:5
Hebrews 9:22; 11:6; 12:14
Revelation 3:20

159. "YESTERDAY'S HISTORY AND TOMORROW'S A MYSTERY"

We shouldn't look to the past unless there are lessons we can learn that will help us in the present. Though we know not how the future will turn out excluding what the Bible says about it, we can rest assured by preparation our lives would be the better for it.

Scripture References
Deuteronomy 5:32-33
Joshua 1:7
Proverbs 4:27
Ezekiel 1:12
Luke 9:62
John 16:13
1st Corinthians 2:9-10; 9:24; 13:8-12
Ephesians 1:9-10
Philippians 3:13
2nd Peter 3:13-14
1st John 3:1-3

160. "THE BRANCH IS STILL SHAKING, BUT THE BIRD HAS FLOWN AWAY"

Any believer who is concerned about their spiritual life will endeavor to maintain the power of God in his life. But when complacency and indifference set in, then attempts to get by on an outward show of piety becomes the norm. Such an individual becomes weak and deceives himself to believe his life is in order with God.

Scripture References
Leviticus 26:36-38
Joshua 7:1-5, 12
Judges 16:16-21
1st Samuel 17:23-24
Isaiah 1:11-15; 29:13; 64:6-7
Matthew 23:23
Mark 9:18-29
Luke 6:46
John 15:1-5
2nd Timothy 3:1-7
Titus 1:16

161. "A ONE-WINGED BIRD CAN'T FLY"

As the saying depicts, just as a bird cannot fly with only one wing and reproduction is not possible without both the woman's egg and man's seed, so it is in the spiritual realm. Jesus describes to Nicodemus in John's third chapter of the need to be born of "water" and "spirit" as the means to enter into the Kingdom of God. It is a baptism or birth from spiritual death to life anew in Jesus Christ, a miracle of regeneration.

Scripture References
Ezekiel 36:26-27
John 1:12-13; 3:3-7
Acts 1:4-5; 10:45-48; 19:1-7
1st Corinthians 15:44-50
2nd Corinthians 5:17
Ephesians 4:4-6
Titus 3:5
Hebrews 6:1-2
James 1:18
1st Peter 1:3-5, 23
1ST John 2:29; 3:9; 5:6

162. "ONCE SAVED, GOD PLACES A RESPONSIBILITY THAT YOU CAN'T GET OUT FROM UNDER"

The Bible speaks of God's redemptive plan for man as that "great salvation". Being recipients of his grace and mercy also carries with it a great responsibility for the child of God. Once we come into the knowledge of the truth we are held accountable for our actions.

Scripture *References*
Matthew 12:36; 18:23-35; 20:1-16, 25-28; 25:1-13
Luke 12:36-40, 42-48
Romans 12:3-9
1st Corinthians 3:4-15; 4:1-5
2nd Corinthians 6:1
Ephesians 6:7
Philippians 2:12
1st Timothy 6:20
2nd Timothy 2:24-26; 4:1-5
Hebrews 12:28-29
James 4:17
1st Peter 4:11

NOTE:
Pentecostal Faith Assembly Church
5347-53 Pulaski Avenue
Philadelphia, PA 19144
www.pfac.cjb.net

Frederick L. Cuthbertson's website:
http://www.ElderFC.com

Bibliographies

(All Scripture references were taken from the Authorized King James Version.)

A number of sayings by Bishop William W. Tucker are variations previously written by other writers. Those quotations are presented here in their original text by the accredited author or sources.

1. "A drop of honey catches more flies than a hogshead of vinegar" (Proverb).

   1666 Torriano, Common Place of Italian Proverbs.

2. "A rolling stone gathers no moss but it gains a certain polish."

   Oliver Herford (1863-1935), U.S. author and illustrator.

3. "Procrastination is the thief of time."

   Edward Young (1683-1765). English Poet and dramatist from "Night Thoughts", "The Complaint", "Night One"
   (1742-46).

4. "Fools rush in where angels fear to tread."

   Alexander Pope (1688-1744). English Poet from "Essay on Criticism."

5. "Marry in haste, we may repent at leisure."

   William Congreve (1670-1729). English dramatist and poet from "The Old Bachelor", Act V, Scene 1.

6. "Honesty is the best policy."

   Miguel de Cervantes (1547-1616). From John Bartlett Familiar Quotations.

7. "They that sleep with dogs shall rise with fleas."

   John Webster (1580-1625). English dramatist. Taken from "The White Devil", Act V, Scene 1.

8. "Give a man enough rope and he'll hang himself" (Proverb).

   Fuller (1639). "Holy War."

9. "As you make your bed, you must lie in it."

   English Proverb borrowed from the Latin and current since the 16th century. Harvey (1590). From "Marginalia."

10. "It is always darkest just before the day dawnest."

    Thomas Fuller from "A Pisgah Sight of Palestine, II" (1650).

11. "Empty wagons make the most noise" (Proverb).

    Lydgate (1430). "Pilgrimage of Man." Early English Text Society.

12. "What you don't know can't hurt you" (Proverb).

    Pettie (1576). "Petite Palace of Pleasure."

13. "Reading is important; read between the lines. Don't swallow everything."

    Gwendolyn Brooks (1917-   ). U.S. poet.

14. "Strike while the iron is hot" (Proverb).

    Chaucer (1386). "Tale of Melibee."

15. "There are three sides to every story: your side, my side, and the right side."

    Spectator Addison (1711). U.S. 1802 Diary and Autobiography of John Adams.

16. "Actions speak louder than words."

    Pym (1628). "Debate on a Message from Charles the First."

17. "Flattery will get you nowhere."

    Box (1954). "Death Likes it Hot."

18. "Curiosity killed the cat."

    Henry (1909). "Schools and Schools."

19. "Don't cut off your nose to spite your face" (Proverb).

    1561. "Deceit of Women."

20. "You can't judge a book by its cover" (Proverb).

    Gardiner (1954). "Murder in Haste." Also 1929 American Speech.

21. "Two wrongs do not make a right."

    Cheales (1875). Proverbial Folklore.

22. "It doesn't amount to a hill of beans."

    Nearo Marsh (1942). "A Man Lay Dead", page 171.

23. "All that glitters is not gold."

   Hali Meidenhad (1220). Early English Text Society.

24. "An honest man's word is as good as his bond."

   Chaucer (1400). "Book of Duchess."

25. "If you dance, you must pay the piper."

   Taylor (1638). "Taylor's Feast."

26. "A dog that will fetch a bone will carry one."

   Forby (1830). "Vocabulary of East Anglia."

27. "Charity begins at home and spreads abroad."

   Wyclif (1380). "Of Prelates in English." Early English Text Society.

28. "Right is right and wrong is wrong."

   Crabbe (first cite 1819). "Tales of the Hall."

29. "It's every man for himself and God for us all."

   Chaucer (first cite 1386). "Knights Tale."

Reference Books

1. A Dictionary of American Proverbs. Oxford University Press, 1992.

2. The Home Book of Proverbs, Maxims and Familiar Phrases. Burton Stevenson, The MacMillan Company, NY, 1959.

3. John Bartlett's Familiar Quotations. Little, Brown and Company, 1992.

4. A New Dictionary of Quotations. H. L. Mencken, New York, 1966.

Acknowledgments

Special thanks go to the Lord Jesus Christ for inspiring me to write this in honor of my mentor, Bishop William W. Tucker. I thank God for bringing these precious sayings back to my remembrance so they can be read and appreciated by all who love God. I honor my wife, Pastor Brenda Cuthbertson for her encouragement to be the best I can be in the Lord.

To my daughters Freda and Melanie, for their patience in "putting up" with me in the use of the computer. To my mother, who raised me in church. Special thanks and gratitude must go to For His Glory Graphic Services for the skills and expertise in putting my writings together and making them presentable. Additional contributions provided by Mother Pauline Tucker. Thanks to Mother Willa Mae Foster, Evangelist Janie English and Mother Louise Green for their help. Also, special thanks to Marion Johnson (Bishop's sister) for her contributions. To Minister Edwin Gregg, thanks for your assistance. Credits also go to my dear brothers and sisters in the Lord who have fellowshipped together with me for years at Bethlehem Temple Apostolic Faith Church, and now at Pentecostal Faith Assembly Church, you know who you are and I thank you very much.